Golf Courses
of the U.S. Open

Golf Courses of the U.S. Open

JOHN STEINBREDER

TAYLOR PUBLISHING COMPANY
DALLAS, TEXAS

PUBLISHED BY TAYLOR PUBLISHING COMPANY
1550 WEST MOCKINGBIRD LANE
DALLAS, TEXAS 75235

FRONTISPIECE: THE SIXTEENTH HOLE AT HAZELTINE NATIONAL GOLF CLUB
(RICHARD HAMILTON SMITH)

DESIGNED BY HESPENHEIDE DESIGN

Library of Congress Cataloging-in-Publication Data

Steinbreder, John.
    Golf courses of the U.S. Open / John Steinbreder.
        p. cm.
    ISBN 0-87833-940-X
    1. Golf Courses—United States—Guidebooks. 2. United States Open
Golf Championship Tournament. I. Title.
GV981.S83 1996
796.352'0973—dc20   96-26094
                                                          CIP

Printed in the United States of America
10 9 8 7 6 5 4 3 2 1

For Exa
and for my golfing buddies, Nat and Pete

Foreword

BY ARNOLD PALMER

I started swinging a golf club when I was three years old and got to play a lot as a youngster, mostly because my father was the head professional and greenskeeper at the Latrobe Country Club in Pennsylvania. I remember when I played as a boy, when I hit balls on the range or practiced my putting, I dreamed of winning a major tournament. My ultimate goal was to beat the field at the U.S. Open. It was the championship of my country, and the winner was considered the best golfer in America.

Another thing that made the Open so appealing was the fact that the tournament had always been played on the top courses of the United States, places like Winged Foot, Merion, Baltusrol, Cherry Hills, Oakmont, The Country Club, and Oakland Hills. They were all great tracks with tremendous style, history, and character, and they provided a superb test of golf without having to resort to any trickery.

Over the years, the U.S. Open has been held at forty-seven different venues, and that number will increase by one when it goes to Pinehurst No. 2 in 1999. Some, such as the Newport Golf Club and the Interlachen Country Club, have hosted the event only once. Others, like Oakmont and Baltusrol, have seen it many times. Different as they may be in terms of layout and location, the courses all have one thing in common: hosting a national championship. This makes them special.

John Steinbreder understands just how special they are, and he has written a wonderful book on the subject. It is a handsome publication that vividly describes how and when the courses were built, who designed them, and what took place during the championships that were decided on their fairways and greens. I have never seen a more complete and colorful book on one of my favorite tournaments—and so many of my favorite courses—and I am sure that golf fans all over the world will enjoy John's work for many years to come.

Acknowledgments

It was the late Harvey Penick who said, "If you play golf, you're my friend," and I found I had plenty of golfing friends as I put together this book. My agent Frank Coffey first got me interested in doing something on the U.S. Open, and he worked up the idea to write about these fine courses with Mike Emmerich of Taylor Publishing. Tony Seidl of TD Media lent a hand along the way, and the three of them kept me going with words of support and encouragement once I got started. My editor, Macy Jaggers, took over after I was finished writing, and she did a first-rate job with my sometimes sloppy prose.

Researching a book of this size and scope was no easy task, and I would have been lost had it not been for the United States Golf Association, its executive director, David Fay, and the registrar of its museum, Nancy Stulack. I'm particularly grateful to Nancy for the long hours she spent pulling course histories and sorting through photographs on my behalf. She also turned me on to some terrific books, and among the

OAK HILL COUNTRY CLUB (ROBERT WALKER)

most useful were *The U.S. Open: Golf's Ultimate Challenge* by Robert Sommers, *Grand Slam Golf* by George Peper and *The Official U.S. Open Almanac,* by Salvatore Johnson. I also spent hours poring over back issues of *Golf Digest, Golf World, Golf,* and *Sports Illustrated* and value the excellent coverage those publications have long given the U.S. Open.

I talked to several former Open champions, and they added a tremendous amount to my knowledge and understanding of that great event and the marvelous courses on which it has been played. Jack Nicklaus, Tom Watson, Billy Casper, Byron Nelson, Hale Irwin, Ken Venturi, and Johnny Miller all took time out from their busy schedules to share their insights, as did Arnold Palmer, who graciously agreed to write the Foreword as well. Thanks, also, to Alastair Johnston, Doc Giffin, Chris Millard, and Chuck Rubin for their help in making some of those players available.

People from a number of the clubs and resorts whose courses are included in this volume sent histories and other useful information my way, and I'd like to thank them as well, especially Owen Costello and Vin Keating of Shinnecock Hills, Andy McGowan of Garden

ix

City, Bob Trebus of Baltusrol, Roberta Nichols of Glen View, Bill Graham of Skokie, Dick Tyska of Midlothian, Douglas Smith of Winged Foot, Geoff Shackelford of Riviera, Donald Kladstrup of Oak Hill, Reed Mackenzie and Irv Fish of Hazeltine, Molly Joest of Pebble Beach, Donna Hand of Atlanta Athletic, Sage Wightman of St. Louis, and Jeanne Taylor of Congressional.

Golf Courses of the U.S. Open contains about 150 photos, many of which came from the USGA archives. But the book also features the work of several top golf photographers, including Larry Lambrecht, Robert Walker, Richard Hamilton Smith, Tom Doak, and Dan McKean. Their pictures have truly brought my words, and the tournament courses, to life. In addition, Sal Johnson provided the U.S. Open statistics and records that are in the boxes with each course.

Although I have loved to play and watch the game for years, I didn't actually begin writing about golf until the fall of 1991. Thanks to a pair of magazine editors, the sport has become a big part of my professional life as well. Robin McMillan of *Met Golfer* handed me my first golf assignment and has kept a steady stream of stories flowing my way ever since. Jerry Tarde of *Golf Digest* has also given me the opportunity to write for his fine magazine, and I've enjoyed working with him and his colleagues Nick Seitz, Roger Schiffman, Chris Hodenfield, Peter McCleery, John Barton, Guy Yocom, and Mike O'Malley. Another golfing friend from *The New York Times* Company is Bob Carney, who has not only let me write for some of his publications but has also provided invaluable help and advice.

I've been working on my own for the past five years and owe a great debt of gratitude to some of the other people who have believed in my abilites as a writer and reporter and given me the chance to make a living doing what I love. Among them are Mark McCormack and Mark Reiter of IMG; Michael Finch and Elaine Armstrong of Rococo International; Roger Toll and Kathleen Ring of *Snow Country*; Bob Brown of *Outdoor Life*, Chuck Wechsler of *Sporting Classics*; Charlie Monagan of *Connecticut Magazine*; Catherine Sabino of *The New York Times* Custom Publishing; and John Walsh, Vince Doria, Jim Cohen, Bob Ley, Sandy Padwe, and Mary Jo Kanser of ESPN. I'm also grateful to Duncan Christy of *Sky*, a first-rate editor who is as good at taking care of his writers as he is at developing quality magazines.

Then, of course, there are those who impact my life in other ways. My mother Cynthia continues to be a wonderful source of support as does Mike Dailey, a dear friend whose heart is as big as a green at Bellerive. I'm also appreciative of the counsel I receive from Bill Creasy and the friendship of my neighbors Arvid and Pam Brandstrom. Thanks, too, to Dick McConn for letting me experience golf in the Kingdom and Eric Purcell, my Bedford partner who makes the trip each July. And finally, here's to my five-year-old daughter Exa, a sweet little girl full of compassion, resilience, and understanding who loves unconditionally, never complains, and is just learning how to swing a golf club.

JOHN STEINBREDER
MAY 1996

Introduction

It is simply the biggest tournament in golf. The British Open may have a more cosmopolitan field, the Masters may have its mystique, and the PGA Championship may be the fourth leg of the game's hallowed Grand Slam, but in terms of competition, toughness, size, and truly determining who the best golfer in the world is each year, none of those tournaments or any other golf event matches the United States Open.

Consider what some of the game's greatest players have to say. "Being an American, the U.S. Open is the championship of my country, and I always looked at it as being the number one tournament that I played," says Jack Nicklaus, whose first professional victory came at the 1962 Open at Oakmont. Billy Casper, the man who won it twice, at Winged Foot in 1959 and Olympic seven years later, feels the same way, "When I started playing the Tour, the U.S. Open was the tournament that I wanted to win more than any other." Adds Hale Irwin, a three-time titlist, "I've always viewed the U.S. Open as the premier golfing event because it lets the best players in the world par-

ticipate. The Masters is a closed shop, the PGA is for the PGA, and not everybody can get over to the British. But the U.S. Open has all the top players in the world." Byron Nelson, who captured the national championship at Philadelphia in 1939, agrees, "I like the Open because it has always had a real strong field. And, of course, it's special because it is held on the best courses in the country."

The courses are one of the things that makes the U.S. Open such a great tournament. From the Newport Golf Club, site of the inaugural Open in 1895, to Southern Hills, which will host the event in the year 2000, from Merion and Oakmont to Shinnecock and Baltusrol, they are the most highly rated layouts in the world. Rich in history and designed by some of golf's most respected architects, these courses represent the best the sport has to offer.

What exactly makes a U.S. Open course? "If you look at the ones on which an Open has been played, you'll find that they are more or less the same," says Nicklaus, who has played in thirty-nine and won four. "They are all older courses on which the rough

MERION GOLF CLUB (ROBERT WALKER)

has been brought in. The golf course is always set up to take the driver out of your hand. Some players don't like it, but that's just the way U.S. Opens are played. The game doesn't have to be played with a driver on every hole, and frankly I like that. The U.S. Open is about patience, about being able to control one's self, about good course management. The Open has never been about power. It has always been about playing the game under the most difficult conditions that the United States Golf Association can give us. And they've given us some pretty difficult conditions over the years."

To Arnold Palmer, a good Open course is one that "gives you the opportunity to play, or at least plan, the good shots without being penalized." Ken Venturi, who won one of the most dramatic Opens in history at Congressional in 1964, believes an Open course must have three essential ingredients: narrow fairways, thick rough, and small, hard greens. "I remember watching Hogan take two shots to get out of the rough and back onto the eighteenth fairway at Olympic," he says. "Some people thought that was a tough break, but that's just the way the Open's supposed to be." Tom Watson, who won at Pebble Beach in 1982, adds, "I've always thought that an Open course should make you use every facet of your game to win. You must drive well, hit your irons well, and putt well."

As would be expected, each of the former champions has their favorite Open course. Many, like Billy Casper, prefer the ones they won on. "I like Winged Foot because it's one of those old, established courses," he says. "It has a lot of sand traps, and you have to drive the ball well to shoot a low score there.

PEBBLE BEACH GOLF LINKS (PEBBLE BEACH COMPANY)

It's also a golf course that lends itself well to Open championships, and you have always had a good player win the tournament there. But I like Olympic even better. It's a great layout and looks so majestic with all those trees."

Venturi and Nelson also consider Olympic their favorite, while Nicklaus and Watson both pick Pebble Beach. Hale Irwin likes the three courses he won his Opens on—Winged Foot, Inverness, and Medinah— but says he is also fond of Olympic and Oakland Hills. "A lot of people like Shinnecock, but I have never felt comfortable on that course," he says. "I've missed the cut both times they've played the Open there." Johnny Miller, on the other hand, loves the venerable Long Island track and says that, if he had his way, the Open would rotate between Shinnecock and Pebble Beach, with a Medinah or Oakmont thrown in every fifth year. Palmer won't pick one favorite, but he lists

Cherry Hills, Oakmont, Winged Foot, and Oakland Hills among his top Open layouts.

There is just as much variance among former champions when it comes to picking the toughest course. Byron Nelson says it was Oakmont in 1935. "I think 299 won the tournament, and the greens were lightning fast," he says. "Back then the course had something like 225 bunkers, and they used these special rakes to create crosswise ridges so you always had to play an explosion shot from the sand." Palmer and Nicklaus both say that the 1963 Open at The Country Club in Brookline, Massachusetts, which Arnold lost in a playoff with Julius Boros and Jack Cupit, was the most difficult they ever saw. "The wind was howling, the rough was high, and the greens were hard as rocks," says Nicklaus, who missed the cut that year. "I think 293 tied for the playoff, which was nine-over." For Tom Watson, the toughest Open track was Oak Hill in Rochester, New York, in 1989. "It didn't have an easy hole," he says. "Most courses give you a break or two along the way, but every par at Oak Hill was a hard par for me."

Some of the players feel the courses they won on were the toughest. "The rough was so heavy at Winged Foot in 1974 and the greens so fast, it was all I could handle to make par," Irwin says. "If you missed a fairway you were almost guaranteed a bogey, or worse. And the course played long that year. You didn't see a lot of wedges being hit." The record shows that Irwin has a valid point; his winning score of 287 was seven over par, and in the years after World War II, only Boros's nine over in 1963 was higher.

Oakmont Country Club (Robert Walker)

Ken Venturi knows how difficult Winged Foot played in 1974 because he was cut after shooting eighty-four and eighty-one. But he thinks the hardest Open course he ever saw was the one on which he captured his only national championship. "Congressional measured nearly 7,100 yards and was probably the longest par seventy in history," he says.

It may not be possible to get a solid consensus from these past winners on which of the Open tracks is the favorite or the toughest. But there certainly is agreement that the courses used for the national championship are among the best in the country. That's why they are worth examining. In the six months I spent researching this book, I found it easy to get caught up in the wonderful stories of how these layouts came to be. I relished the tales of Charles Blair Macdonald building the country's first eighteen-hole course at the Chicago Golf Club in 1895, of the Shriners who created Medinah just before the stock market crash of 1929, and of the man who decided to

found Shinnecock Hills after watching a golf exhibition while on vacation in France more than a century ago. I also liked reliving the great moments in Open tournament history, from twenty-year-old Francis Ouimet stunning the golfing world in 1913 with his playoff win at The Country Club over Harry Vardon and Ted Ray to Hale Irwin high-fiving the greenside gallery after sinking a forty-five-foot birdie on the seventy-second hole in 1990 to force the play-off he won the next day. These courses and competitions captivated me, and I came away with an enormous appreciation for the visionaries who designed and built the tracks, for the men and women who kept them going over the years, and for the players who battled such extraordinary pressures to win a U.S. Open title. It was a fascinating journey, and I hope you enjoy the ride as much as I did.

Golf Courses of the U.S. Open

Atlanta Athletic Club

1976

The letter arrived at United States Golf Association headquarters in mid-November 1971 and read, in part, "Our membership is most eager to be awarded . . . the USGA Open Championship . . . and I should be most happy if my old club should become the host for my favorite golf tournament." It was signed by Bobby Jones, and the club he was referring to was Atlanta Athletic, the place where he first honed his masterful swing. Not surprisingly, the USGA honored the request and voted to hold an Open there. But Jones, a frail man of sixty-nine who had

EARLY IN HIS CAREER, GOLF LEGEND BOBBY JONES HONED HIS SWING AT ATLANTA ATHLETIC CLUB. A MONTH BEFORE HIS DEATH IN 1972, HE REQUESTED THAT THE USGA AWARD AN OPEN TO HIS OLD CLUB. IN JONES'S HONOR, THE OPEN CAME TO ATLANTA IN 1976. (ATLANTA ATHLETIC CLUB)

FOUR DIFFERENT ARCHITECTS CONTRIBUTED TO THE DESIGN OF THE 1976 OPEN COURSE; ROBERT TRENT JONES AND JOHN FINGER DID THE ORIGINAL WORK WHILE GEORGE AND TOM FAZIO TOUGHENED IT UP FOR THE EVENT WITH BUNKERS LIKE THESE.

(ATLANTA ATHLETIC CLUB)

been ravaged by a crippling spinal disease called syringomyelia, died before the decision was handed down.

Actually, the layout on which the 1976 Open would be held was a good twenty-five miles away from the track that Jones had played as a boy. Atlanta's old course, known as East Lake, was sold by the members in 1968, with the proceeds going toward the construction of a grand thirty-six-hole facility near the Chattahoochee River in Duluth. The course was designed by Robert Trent Jones, who built twenty-seven of the holes, and John Finger, who constructed the remaining nine. The USGA decided to use Finger's nine as the outward half of the Open track and one of Trent Jones's nine as the inward. They also suggested that the club revamp several sections of the course. The members responded by hiring architects George and Tom Fazio, and the uncle-nephew team remodeled every bunker, built fifteen new tees, and cut six greens back in size. The Fazios also changed the pars on three holes: the eleventh became a monstrous 480-yard par four, the twelfth was transformed from a long par four into a par five, and the par five eighteenth was converted into a tough par four finisher with a large pond guarding the green.

The whole course played tough the first day of the tournament, and only amateur Mike Reid, who shot a sixty-seven, managed to break par. Many of the contestants complained that the fairway grass was too long and said they couldn't get proper spin on the ball. Tournament officials inspected their mowers and found that the blades were indeed one-quarter inch too high. The fairways were recut by the start of play the following morning, and big names started to creep onto the leader board. John Mahaffey was up by a stroke after thirty-six holes and increased his lead to two on Saturday when he carded a sixty-nine. But he lost that advantage Sunday. After three-putting seventeen, he found himself one shot behind his playing partner, a twenty-two-year-old Tour rookie and former U.S. Amateur champion named Jerry Pate.

There was, however, one more hole to play. Pate and Mahaffey both pushed their drives into the rough. Mahaffey pulled out a four wood and tried to muscle his second shot to the green from a brutal lie. But it fell short and splashed into the pond. Pate's ball, on the other hand, sat up nicely on a tuft of grass. He took a five iron and hit what many consider one of the finest shots in Open history, a 190-yarder to within two feet. Pate tapped in for birdie and won his only Open title by two

THANKS TO A MAJOR REDESIGN BY ARNOLD PALMER AND ED SEAY IN 1988, THE COURSE AT ATLANTA HAS CHANGED DRAMATICALLY SINCE JERRY PATE'S 1976 OPEN WIN. (ATLANTA ATHLETIC CLUB)

strokes. Tied for second were a pair of veterans, Al Geiberger and Tom Weiskopf. Mahaffey ended up three back and tied for fourth.

Atlanta has never hosted another U.S. Open, but it has had its share of majors over the years. It has been the site of the 1981 PGA, the 1984 Mid-Amateur, and the 1990 Women's Open. The championship course, which is known as Highlands, was redesigned by Arnold Palmer and Ed Seay in 1988 and is significantly different from the track on which Jerry Pate prevailed. But it remains a splendid place to play golf and reminisce about the shot-making—and letter-writing—abilities of the club's most famous member, Bobby Jones.

Baltimore Country Club

1899

ALTHOUGH BALTIMORE COUNTRY CLUB'S ROLAND PARK COURSE NO LONGER EXISTS, THE CLUB STILL MAINTAINS THE CLUBHOUSE AND FIRST HOLE MUCH AS IT LOOKED HERE CIRCA 1899. (BALTIMORE COUNTRY CLUB)

The Baltimore Country Club didn't waste any time getting itself a U.S. Open. Founded in 1898, it hosted the national championship the following year on the Roland Park course designed by Willie Dunn. Another pair of Willies—Smith and Anderson—shot seventy-seven to share the first-round lead. Anderson carded an eighty-one to go up by

one after thirty-six holes, but then the twenty-four-year-old Smith
slowly pulled away. He built a four-shot lead after posting a seventy-
nine in the third round, and when he finished with a seventy-seven he
was eleven strokes ahead of his nearest competitors. His record still
stands as the largest margin of victory in Open history.

It was not an easy tournament for many of the players. Anderson
shot eighty-five in the third round, for example, to fall out of contention. A nineteen-year-old Scotsman named Alex Campbell stood just
four strokes off the pace at the start of the final eighteen, thanks in part
to a thirty-five he had carded on the front nine that morning. But he
could manage only a forty-four on that same loop in the afternoon and
then took a ten on the fifteenth when he had trouble extricating his ball
from a ditch. He ended up with a ninety-four, which put him out of the
money in twelfth place. H.V. Hoare, a professional from Dayton, Ohio,
broke ninety only once and finished even lower, tied for forty-second;
but he did win a pretournament driving contest and a twenty dollar
prize. Even Smith had his share of problems; he drove his ball into a
ditch in front of the tenth tee three out of four times and never made
better than six on the hole.

SCOTSMAN WILLIE DUNN DESIGNED
BALTIMORE'S ROLAND PARK COURSE,
WHICH WAS SOLD TO DEVELOPERS IN
1963. (USGA)

Roland Park was one of three golf courses the Baltimore Country Club eventually built, with the other two being added in 1924 on property some twenty miles away. One of those courses, Five Farms, was designed by A.W. Tillinghast and later hosted the 1928 PGA Championship, the 1932 U.S. Amateur, the 1965 Walker Cup, and the 1988 U.S. Women's Open. In the early 1960s the club sold the original Roland Park property to developers, and the last rounds were played there in 1963. Baltimore did keep the old stone clubhouse at Roland Park as its headquarters, however, and still maintains the first hole, which looks almost exactly as it did back in 1899. Outlines of the old seventeenth and eighteenth can be seen as well, and on the first tee is a plaque commemorating Smith's victory.

Willie Smith never won another Open, but he finished in the top ten the next four years in a row. His older brother, Alex, captured two national championships, in 1906 and 1910, and his younger brother, Macdonald, came close on several occasions himself. After working as a pro at Midlothian Country Club in Illinois for a while, Willie Smith took a job at a course in Mexico City. Unfortunately, he got caught in the cross-fire of the Mexican Revolution and was killed while hiding out in the basement of his pro shop as the club was being shelled. He was only forty years old.

BUILT IN 1898, BALTIMORE COUNTRY CLUB'S ROLAND PARK COURSE HOSTED THE U.S. OPEN THE FOLLOWING YEAR. WILLIE SMITH TOOK THE TITLE WITH AN ELEVEN-STROKE LEAD—THE LARGEST IN OPEN HISTORY. (BALTIMORE COUNTRY CLUB)

Baltusrol Golf Club

1903, 1915, 1936, 1954, 1967, 1980, 1993

Baltusrol has hosted seven U.S. Opens over the years and is rightfully considered one of the top courses in the United States. It is also the only golf club with the unique distinction of being named after a murder.

The killing occurred on Washington's Birthday in 1831. A farmer named Baltus Roll lived outside the New Jersey town of Springfield, and one evening two men broke into his house, dragged him outside, tied him up, and beat him to death. Then they ransacked his home, but left after finding nothing of value. Police suspected robbery as the motive and later arrested two men. One, a local innkeeper, was acquitted on a technicality, while the other, a drifter, committed suicide.

Sixty-four years after the murder that some New Yorkers called "the crime of the century," Louis Keller, a wealthy gentleman farmer and the publisher of the *Social Register*, bought the old Roll property, hired Englishman George Hunter to design a nine-hole course, and started a golf club. When it was finished, the track measured 2,372 yards, with only two of the holes being longer than three hundred yards. It was

THE ORIGINAL BALTUSROL CLUBHOUSE WAS DESTROYED IN A 1909 FIRE. ITS REPLACEMENT WAS BUILT OVERLOOKING THE PERILOUS BUNKER ON THE EIGHTEENTH GREEN OF THE ORIGINAL COURSE. (BALTUSROL GOLF CLUB)

JACK NICKLAUS HAS ENJOYED GREAT
SUCCESS ON THE LOWER COURSE,
WINNING TWO OF HIS FOUR OPEN TITLES
THERE. IN 1967, HE SMASHED THE
RECORD WITH A 275, BEATING OUT
ARNOLD PALMER. THIRTEEN YEARS
LATER HE BROKE HIS OWN RECORD WITH
A 272 IN A SHOWDOWN WITH JAPAN'S
ISAO AOKI. (BALTUSROL GOLF CLUB)

Keller who hit upon the idea of calling his new club Baltusrol, after the farmer who had been killed on the land, and his creation became so popular that he added another nine holes in 1897 to ease overcrowding.

In 1901, Baltusrol hosted the Women's Amateur and two years later had its first U.S. Open. The winner was Willie Anderson, a Scotsman who had been the club's head professional in 1898 and 1899. He shot a then-record seventy-three in the first round and hung on to beat David Brown in a play-off. It was Anderson's second U.S. Open title, and he would go on to win the next two. No one would ever break his record of four national championships, although Bobby Jones, Ben Hogan, and Jack Nicklaus each would tie it. The Open returned to Baltusrol in 1915, and the winner this time was Jerome Travers. A four-time U.S. Amateur champion, he took a job as a cotton broker on Wall Street shortly after his victory and became the only player never to defend his Open title.

The next championship didn't come to Baltusrol until 1936, and it took place on an entirely different course. Shortly after Travers's win, Keller had begun to feel that his club needed another layout and asked A.W. Tillinghast if he would design a new course. Tillie agreed but added that the original course was becoming obsolete and suggested

that it be completely done over as well. The membership approved the plan, and the architect went right to work, building what became known as the Upper Course on the side of one of the Watchung Mountains and the Lower Course on flatter, more open terrain. Both courses opened for play in 1922.

The 1936 Open was held on the par seventy-two, 6,866-yard Upper Course, and the surprise winner was Tony Manero, a driving range pro and the son of a Yonkers grocer. Manero shot a blistering sixty-seven for his final round to beat "Lighthorse" Harry Cooper by two strokes. The championship moved to the Lower Course in 1954, the first year that the Open was nationally televised, and Ed Furgol battled Gene Littler and several other players over four difficult rounds before coming out on top by one stroke with a 284.

Jack Nicklaus won the next two Opens at Baltusrol, both of which were held on the par seventy, 7,000-yard Lower Course. The first one, in 1967, featured a classic duel between the Golden Bear and the King, Arnold Palmer. They had been tied after fifty-four holes and played the final day together. Arnold shot sixty-nine, but Jack countered with a

WHEN ROBERT TRENT JONES REDESIGNED THE PAR-THREE FOURTH HOLE ON BALTUSROL'S LOWER COURSE, MEMBERS COMPLAINED THAT THE WATER WAS TOO DIFFICULT TO CLEAR. JONES SILENCED THE PROTESTS BY ACING THE HOLE WITH A FIVE-IRON THE FIRST TIME HE PLAYED IT. AFTERWARD HE DECLARED, "GENTLEMEN, I THINK THE HOLE IS EMINENTLY FAIR." (BALTUSROL GOLF CLUB)

EVEN THOUGH THE PAR-FIVE
SEVENTEENTH MEASURED 617 YARDS AT
THE 1995 OPEN, JOHN DALY MANAGED
TO REACH THE GREEN IN A RECORD TWO.
(BALTUSROL GOLF CLUB)

dazzling sixty-five, birding the final hole with a white-faced putter he had borrowed earlier in the week from future PGA commissioner Deane Beman. In capturing his second U.S. Open title, Nicklaus had also broken Ben Hogan's seventy-two-hole record with a sizzling 275.

Nicklaus did even better in 1980. At forty years old and with only one major win in the past five years, he was not among the betting favorites. Some observers had speculated that Jack's best days were behind him, but Nicklaus quickly proved the doubters wrong by opening with a sixty-three. He followed that with rounds of seventy-one, seventy, and sixty-eight for a 272 and another Open record. His chief competition came from Japan's Isao Aoki, with whom he was tied after fifty-four holes. Nicklaus built a two-stroke lead after nine the final day, but he could not shake his determined foe. At ten, he hit his approach to three feet for a certain birdie, but Aoki answered by chipping in for a birdie of his own. Nicklaus parred the next six holes, but so did Aoki. At the par-five seventeenth, Nicklaus was lying three, twenty-two feet away from the pin, while Aoki, who hit his approach stiff, had only a five-footer for birdie. But Jack drained his putt, and as it hit the hole he raised his putter into the air, danced a little jig, and smiled broadly in a picture that has been splashed across a dozen magazine and book covers. A routine birdie at eighteen gave him Open win number four. The sign on the huge eighteenth-hole scoreboard said it best: "Jack Is Back."

Jack did go back to Baltusrol for the 1993 Open, but he was never in the mix and finished tied for seventy-second with a 289. The victor this time was twenty-eight-year-old Lee Janzen, who displayed unusual fortitude in winning his first major by hanging on to an Open lead for three days and tying Nicklaus's seventy-two-hole record in the process. Another record was set that year when John Daly reached the 617-yard seventeenth hole in two. After a drive of some 325 yards, Daly whacked a one iron onto the green and then two-putted for his bird.

Baltusrol isn't yet on the schedule for another Open, but it would be hard to imagine the club not getting its eighth before long. Perhaps 2006 is the most likely date because it will have been thirteen years from its last Open, and since 1954, the Open has come to Baltusrol every thirteen years.

Bellerive Country Club

1965

Bellerive was only a baby when it hosted the 1965 National Championship. Designed by Robert Trent Jones, it had opened on Memorial Day weekend five years before. The track ran nearly 7,200 yards and was the longest in Open history, with six of its par fours exceeding 450 yards.

The effort to build Bellerive was led by Hord Hardin, a St. Louis banker who later served as president of the United States Golf Association and chairman of Augusta National. A talented player who had reached the semifinals of the 1949 Western Amateur, he was among a large group of St. Louis Field Club members who felt their old course, which had been designed in 1908 by Robert Foulis of St. Andrews, was past its prime. So in the mid-1950s they orchestrated the purchase of some 350 acres of farmland to the west of the city. Hardin hired Jones

to construct a new course, and the architect sculpted a first-rate track out of the Missouri countryside with wide fairways, plenty of bunkers, and enormous greens.

But would it be ready for an Open so soon? Hardin thought so, and with St. Louis poised to celebrate its bicentennial in 1965, he approached his friends at the USGA about staging their signature event at his club. They listened carefully to the man who also happened to be a member of the organization's executive committee and eventually agreed to alter their schedule; instead of taking the 1965 championship to Olympic in San Francisco, they would push that course back a year and bring the Open to Bellerive instead.

To many observers, Bellerive showed its immaturity from the beginning. A number of the trees on the new course were still saplings, and the grass on one of the fairways had not yet knitted together. Bellerive also came under criticism for the size of its greens, which some people claimed were turning the Open into a putting contest because they were so easy to hit.

But Gary Player didn't have any complaints. The powerful South African carded a pair of seventies the first two days and was one shot up on Kel Nagle and Mason Rudolph after thirty-six holes. Saturday that year was going to be easier than in Opens past because the

GARY PLAYER'S 1965 OPEN VICTORY AT
BELLERIVE MADE HIM THE THIRD PLAYER
IN HISTORY TO HAVE WON ALL FOUR OF
THE MAJOR PROFESSIONAL TITLES. JACK
NICKLAUS JOINED HIM IN THAT
DISTINCTION WITH A BRITISH OPEN WIN
THE FOLLOWING YEAR. (PAT SEELIG)

tournament was being played for the first time over four days, not three. Part of the reason for the additional day was the frightening sight of Ken Venturi staggering home after thirty-six holes at Congressional the previous year. But perhaps an even larger consideration was television, which liked the idea of presenting shows on both Saturday and Sunday.

Player posted a one-over-par seventy-one in the third round and remained on top by two strokes over Nagle and Frank Beard. He continued playing well on Sunday and was three up with three holes to play. Then he double-bogeyed the par-three sixteenth while Nagle, playing one hole ahead, birdied, and suddenly the two men were tied, which is how they would finish the day.

A play-off was held the following afternoon, and Player showed up in the same black shirt he had been wearing all week, having washed it each evening in his hotel room. He jumped off to a quick lead, going two up after three holes, and shot seventy-one to Nagle's seventy-four. The victory made Player the first foreigner to win the Open since Englishman Ted Ray at Inverness in 1920, and with the title he joined Jack Nicklaus, Ben Hogan, and Gene Sarazen as the only men ever to win all four of the modern Grand Slam events.

THE USGA BROKE WITH TRADITION WHEN IT AWARDED THE OPEN TO A YOUNG CLUB, FIVE-YEAR-OLD BELLERIVE, IN 1965. (BELLERIVE COUNTRY CLUB)

Player received $25,000 for his victory and, in an extraordinary gesture, donated his share of the purse to charity, with $5,000 going to cancer research and the balance to the USGA for the promotion of junior golf.

Brae Burn Country Club

1919

The Brae Burn Country Club in West Newtown, Massachusetts, was one of the first courses Donald Ross ever designed. It was also a favorite of the great Scottish architect, and he was still tinkering with the layout in 1947, the year before he died. It was one of the last courses he ever worked on.

Built in 1898, Brae Burn was the venue for the 1906 and 1975 Women's Amateurs (won by Harriet Curtis and Beth Daniel, respectively), the 1928 U.S. Amateur (captured by Bobby Jones), and the 1958 and 1970 Curtis Cup. The 6,375-yard, par-seventy-one course was also

WALTER HAGEN CAPTURED THE 1919 OPEN AT BRAE BURN DESPITE POSTING A DOUBLE-BOGEY FIVE IN THE PLAYOFF ON THE 225-YARD SEVENTEENTH, PICTURED HERE AROUND THAT TIME. (USGA)

the site of the 1919 U.S. Open, the first national championship since the event was suspended in 1916 due to World War I. Instead of having qualifying rounds, the United States Golf Association decided to play each of the first two rounds on single days. A Bostonian named Mike Brady had the lead after thirty-six holes, and a third-round seventy-three gave him a five-stroke advantage over Walter Hagen heading into the final eighteen.

But that lead quickly disappeared as Brady suffered a bad case of the jitters and staggered to an eighty. Playing nearly an hour behind him, Hagen shot thirty-eight on the front and, after a bogey on twelve, parred thirteen through seventeen. He hit a tremendous mashie with his second shot at eighteen to within ten feet, and as he walked to the green he sent a spectator into the clubhouse to fetch Brady, saying, "He should see this." Hagen would win if he sank his putt, and with Brady watching, he stroked the ball right at the hole. But it spun off the lip, and when Hagen knocked in his par, the two men were deadlocked at 301.

The play-off was held the following day. Legend has it that Hagen spent most of the evening before partying with Al Jolson and never

BRAE BURN, SHOWN HERE FROM THE FIRST GREEN WITH THE CLUBHOUSE IN THE DISTANCE, WAS LAID OUT IN 1898 BY DONALD ROSS. THE COURSE WAS ONE OF THE FIRST ROSS DESIGNED, AND HE CONTINUED TO MAKE MINOR MODIFICATIONS OVER THE NEXT FORTY-FIVE YEARS. (USGA)

went to bed. Brady parred the first hole but took a six on the second to fall one back and was never able to make up the difference, losing seventy-seven to seventy-eight. It was Hagen's second, and last, Open win.

Scotsman Willie Chisholm withdrew after the opening round, but he still managed to set an Open record—for most strokes taken on a single hole—when he carded an eighteen on the par-three eighth. Chisholm, it seems, had sent his ball into a rocky ravine that fronted the green, and it took him nearly thirty minutes to get it out. Somewhere along the way, the story goes, he lost count of how many strokes he had taken and asked his playing partner Jim Barnes for help. "You had an eighteen," Barnes said to him. "Oh, Jim, that can't be," Chisholm replied. "You must have been counting the echoes." (Amazingly, an obscure California pro named Ray Ainsley broke that record in 1938 when he took a nineteen on the sixteenth hole at Cherry Hills; his total score for the day was ninety-six.)

Country Club of Buffalo

1912

Time stands still at the Country Club of Buffalo, and no where is that more apparent than on the golf course. Designed by Donald Ross in the early 1900s and touched up in later years by Robert Trent Jones and Geoffrey Cornish, it has changed little since hosting the 1912 U.S. Open.

The tournament was played in early August that year, and it pitted defending champion John McDermott against a field of 127 golfers, almost twice as many as had competed in the Open at Chicago the year before. Some players were going off on the par seventy-four, 6,300-yard track as early as 6:30 a.m., and since the tournament consisted of two rounds a day, many of them were just finishing at nightfall. Not surprisingly, McDermott was the favorite. A Philadelphia native who had left home before completing high school to work as a professional at the Atlantic City Country Club, he was an extraordinary talent. He was only seventeen when he competed in his first U.S. Open (at Englewood in 1909), eighteen when he came in second at the Philadelphia Cricket Club in 1910, and nineteen when he won for the first time, making him the youngest player—and the only teenager—to ever capture the national title.

THE COURSE AT THE COUNTRY CLUB OF
BUFFALO—THE PAR-THREE SIXTH HOLE
IS SHOWN HERE IN THE EARLY 1900S—
WAS DESIGNED BY DONALD ROSS. IT HAS
CHANGED LITTLE SINCE JOHN
MCDERMOTT WON THE OPEN THERE IN
1912. (USGA)

McDermott played well the first day at Buffalo, shooting seventy-four and seventy-five for a score of 149 that left him tied with two other golfers two strokes off the pace. But he started badly the following morning, hitting two balls out of bounds on number one and then scrambling to a bogey on the second. He finally managed to collect himself, and played the remaining holes three under par—including an eagle on the 606-yard tenth, the only par-six in Open history—to post with another seventy-four, three shots off the lead but still in good position for the final eighteen.

McDermott's main competition was Mike Brady, who was one of the men he had beaten in the playoff at Chicago the previous year. But Brady stumbled early on, and McDermott caught him after only two holes to take the lead after three. He was two under after nine and seemed to be cruising when a Bostonian named Tom McNamara started tearing up the course. Playing in the group ahead of McDermott, he had birdied three of the first four holes on the back nine and came home in thirty-four, giving himself a sixty-nine for the round and a seventy-two-hole total of 296. The defending champ was on the fifteenth hole when McNamara walked off eighteen, and he responded by birdieing

the par-three sixteenth and parring seventeen. A bogey at the last hole did him no harm, and McDermott took the Open again, edging McNamara by two shots.

It seemed that McDermott could do no wrong on the golf course after that win, but he would play in only two more Opens, finishing eighth the following year and tied for ninth in 1914. A series of personal mishaps led to an emotional breakdown in 1915, and sadly, McDermott spent the rest of his years in and out of institutions. He never played in another tournament.

DESPITE A BOGEY ON THE LAST HOLE, JOHN McDERMOTT, THE YOUNGEST PLAYER EVER TO WIN A U.S. OPEN, CLAIMED HIS SECOND CONSECUTIVE NATIONAL TITLE BY TWO STROKES AT BUFFALO. (USGA)

Canterbury Golf Club

1940, 1946

Founded in 1922, the Canterbury Golf Club in Shaker Heights, Ohio was named after the English town in which Moses Cleveland, the founder of the state's biggest city, was born. The 6,900-yard, par-seventy-two course was designed by Herbert Strong, and it has hosted two dramatic U.S. Opens, both of which were decided by play-offs.

WHEN GENE SARAZEN HEARD THAT HE
NEEDED A THIRTY-FOUR ON THE FINAL
ROUND BACK NINE TO TIE LAWSON
LITTLE IN THE 1940 OPEN, HE BIRDIED
THE ELEVENTH HOLE, SHOWN HERE, AS
WELL AS THE THIRTEENTH TO FORCE THE
PLAY-OFF. (ROBERT WALKER)

The first one took place in 1940, and it featured another patented collapse by Sam Snead. One shot off the pace going into the final round, he carded an eighty-one and fell into a discouraging tie for sixteenth. Several other players, however, did well that day, among them Lawson Little, who finished with a seventy-two-hole score of 287 and went into the clubhouse with the lead. Gene Sarazen had just completed the front nine when he heard about Little's score and knew he needed to shoot thirty-four on the back to tie. And that's just what he did, posting birdies at eleven and thirteen and forcing a play-off. A third player, Ed "Porky" Oliver, also recorded a 287, but he was disqualified for playing out of turn. Earlier that day, Oliver and several other golfers had seen a storm developing and rushed out to the first tee so they could get in their rounds before the rain. But the starter, Joe Dey of the United

States Golf Association, was having lunch in the clubhouse at the time. The marshal on hand warned the players not to hit until they had spoken to Dey. But they went off anyway, and all paid the price. Oliver was devastated when he heard the news, and he cried openly in the locker room. Little and Sarazen argued that Oliver should be included in the play-off, but the USGA would not bend. Little, who had won the U.S. and British Amateurs in 1934 and 1935, surged ahead by three at the turn, and even though Sarazen eventually pulled to within one, he never let go of his lead.

The USGA suspended the Open after the 1941 event as a result of World War II and didn't hold the championship again until 1946, when it returned to Canterbury. Byron Nelson led going into the final round, but he bogeyed the last two holes and finished in a tie with Lloyd Mangrum and Vic Ghezzi. The three men matched seventy-twos in a play-off the following morning and then went back out for a second round in the afternoon. Nelson and Ghezzi were tied after twelve holes,

TWO MONTHS AFTER THE 1946 OPEN AT CANTERBURY, BYRON NELSON, WHO LOST THE OPEN TO LLOYD MANGRUM BY ONE IN A PLAY-OFF, ANNOUNCED HIS RETIREMENT FROM PROFESSIONAL GOLF. (ROBERT WALKER)

and Mangrum stood three back. But he made a couple of quick birdies and managed to beat Ghezzi and Nelson each by a stroke. Nelson was only thirty-four years old at the time, but Canterbury would be his last Open. The pressures of the game were getting to him, and he retired to his ranch in Roanoke, Texas.

Canterbury hasn't had another Open since, but it has hosted other majors over the years, including the 1964 and 1979 U.S. Amateurs. It was also the site of the 1973 PGA Championship, which was won by Ohio's own Jack Nicklaus.

Champions Golf Club

1969

Jimmy Demaret and Jack Burke, Jr., grew up in Houston, Texas, and they had long dreamed of building a championship golf course in their hometown. They considered several ideas over the years, and in 1958 finally put a plan into action. Working with designer Ralph Plummer, they constructed two eighteen-hole layouts and founded the Champions Golf Club. Both courses earned high praise from the golfing public, with the one known as Cypress Creek getting most of the accolades. Cypress Creek soon became the home of the Houston Open, and in 1967 it also hosted the Ryder Cup matches. Two years later, it was the site of an even bigger event, the U.S. Open.

Lee Trevino had won the national championship at Oak Hill in Rochester, New York, the year before. When he arrived in Houston in the summer of 1969, everyone wanted to know who he thought would win that year's tournament, provided, of course, that he did not repeat.

THE FOURTH HOLE ON CHAMPIONS' CYPRESS CREEK COURSE LEADS PLAYERS AROUND A MENACING WATER HAZARD THAT COMES INTO PLAY ON SEVERAL HOLES. (USGA)

Golf Courses of the U.S. Open

"Orville Moody," Trevino replied. "Why him?" people asked. "Because," Trevino said, "he is one hell of a player."

Even though Moody had been knocking around the PGA Tour for a couple of years, not many people knew about him. But Trevino had met the Oklahoma native when they were both serving overseas in the military and thought a lot of his game. And with good reason. Moody, affectionately known as "Sarge," could strike the ball as well as anyone, and in addition to winning the Korean Open three times during his fourteen-year military career, he had also captured the All-Services title in 1965. But he had problems with his putting, and that part of his game had gotten so bad that he barely qualified for the Open at Champions.

Moody posted a seventy-one for his first round and was tied with twelve others in fourteenth place. It was a solid effort but gave no reason to believe that Trevino had a future in fortune-telling. That began to change, however, when a second-day seventy brought the former

DESPITE THE UNLIKELIHOOD OF LEE TREVINO'S PREDICTION, ORVILLE MOODY WAS A SURPRISE WINNER AT THE 1969 OPEN. (PAT SEELIG)

Army sergeant up into a fifth-place tie. After he fired a sixty-eight on Saturday, Moody climbed into second, three back of Miller Barber, who would be his playing partner for the final eighteen.

Barber started badly on Sunday, bogeying five of the first eight holes and letting a slew of players back into the tournament. Sarge made only one bogey during that stretch and found himself in the lead at the end of the front nine. He played steadily the rest of the day, watching Barber fall out completely, hearing about Arnold Palmer and Al Geiberger making moves, and worrying about the scores that Deane Beman, Bob Rosburg, Bruce Crampton, and other competitors were carding. Moody wasn't sure where he stood on the 18th tee, but he hit a strong drive and put his approach shot 14 feet from the pin. As soon as he reached the green, he went up to Frank Hannigan, a United States Golf Association official, and asked what the low score was. Hannigan simply replied, "You have two putts for the championship."

Moody lined up his first putt and stroked it to within a foot. Then he tapped in for his par and his only U.S. Open title. He would never win another official Tour event, but he would go on to capture a dozen different championships on the Seniors Tour. And he would forever make it seem that Lee Trevino could read a crystal ball as well as a bent-grass green.

Cherry Hills Country Club

1938, 1960, 1978

Cherry Hills will forever be known as Arnold Palmer's course, and not because he and his partner Ed Seay redesigned the Englewood, Colorado, track in 1977. It is considered his course because in 1960 he staged the greatest comeback in U.S. Open history there, charging from a seven-stroke deficit at the start of the final round to capture his only Open title by two shots over Jack Nicklaus. Palmer did it by driving the green on the 346-yard, par-four first hole and then two-putting for birdie; he did it by chipping in for another bird on two, by tapping in for yet one more on three and by draining an eighteen-footer for a three on the par-four fourth. He seemed to come back to earth for a moment

when he parred five, but then Arnie quickly reeled off two more birds at six and seven. He ended up tying an Open record by shooting thirty on the front side, and then carded a one-under-par thirty-five on the back nine for his win.

Although the 1960 Open truly was Palmer's tournament, it had other special moments as well. It was the last time that forty-seven-year-old Ben Hogan seriously competed for a national championship. The Hawk opened on Thursday with a seventy-five but then posted stellar rounds of sixty-seven and sixty-nine to stand only three shots back after fifty-four holes. Unfortunately, he could shoot no better than seventy-three for his final eighteen, dumping balls into the water on seventeen and eighteen and finishing tied for ninth, four shots off the pace.

It was also the first time Jack Nicklaus threatened to win a major. The twenty-year-old Ohio native, who was playing as an amateur, more than held his own with rounds of seventy-one, seventy-one, sixty-nine, and seventy-one for a seventy-two-hole total of 282. In fact, no amateur has ever scored so well in an Open. But Nicklaus had yet to learn the secret of winning majors, and that was evident when he missed a couple

THE STEEP SLOPES OF THE HIGH-ALTITUDE ENGLEWOOD, COLORADO, COURSE, ALONG WITH ITS PLENTIFUL WATER HAZARDS, WERE TO BLAME FOR RAY AINSLEY'S RECORD-BREAKING SCORE OF NINETEEN AT THE 1939 OPEN—THE HIGHEST EVER ON A SINGLE HOLE IN AN OPEN. (ROBERT WALKER)

WHEN FIRST OPENED IN 1922, CHERRY HILLS WAS ALMOST COMPLETELY DEVOID OF TREES. ASIDE FROM A GENTLE REMODEL OF THE COURSE BY ARNOLD PALMER AND ED SEAY IN 1977, THE GROWTH OF THOUSANDS OF TREES IS ABOUT THE ONLY THING THAT'S CHANGED. (ROBERT WALKER)

of short putts on the final eighteen. He impressed nonetheless, and his playing partner that final day, Ben Hogan, had this to say about the prodigy: "I played thirty-six holes today with a kid who should have won this thing by ten strokes."

Hogan was only a kid himself when the Cherry Hills Country Club opened for business in 1922. It was started by a group of men from the Denver Country Club who felt their old haunt had become too crowded. They wanted to step out on their own, and after buying some land just south of the Colorado capital, they hired William Flynn to build a course. And that he did, constructing a championship-caliber track that was practically devoid of trees. Cherry Hill struggled through its early years, and then the Depression hit, nearly sending it into bankruptcy. The club fathers thought a major tournament might help reverse their fortunes and, in 1937, approached the United States Golf Association about holding the Open there the following year. The USGA consented, but knowing that Cherry Hills had financial problems, demanded a $10,000 bond to assure that the club would not go broke in the process.

By all accounts, the 1938 Open was a grand success. Ralph Guldahl won his second straight national championship, rebounding from a four-stroke deficit at the start of the final round to win by six. The tournament attracted strong crowds, ensuring that it would be an economic success and giving the club a much-needed financial boost.

ARNOLD PALMER TIED OLIN DUTRA'S RECORD SET AT THE 1934 OPEN WHEN HE CAME BACK FROM EIGHT STROKES DOWN TO WIN THE OPEN IN 1960. (PAT SEELIG)

Moneywise, Cherry Hills was in much better shape when it hosted a third Open forty years later. But the course had needed a little work. Even at seven thousand-plus yards, it had always been on the shortish side for pros hitting balls in Englewood's rarefied air. So the club toughened it up for the championship. The man in charge of the redesign was Arnold Palmer, and one of the first things he did was increase the yardage on the fabled first hole by more than fifty yards. No one would be driving that green in 1978.

Hale Irwin led after the first round, but Andy North was on top after two. The lanky Wisconsin native sunk a monstrous forty-five-foot birdie putt to close out his third round with a seventy-one and held a one-shot advantage over Gary Player. North played the front in even par that final day but ran into some troubles on the back. He took a double bogey on the par three fifteenth, but when he stepped to the eighteenth

tee, he was still two strokes ahead of his closest competitors, all of whom were already in the clubhouse.

That lead barely held up. North pushed his drive into the rough on eighteen, pulled his second shot into more rough, and then chunked a wedge into a greenside bunker. He blasted out of the sand to four feet and needed only to sink the putt for the win. Twice he stood over his ball, and twice he stepped away, mostly because of a strong wind that was blowing in his face. Then he calmly stroked it into the cup.

Chicago Golf Club

1897, 1900, 1911

Few clubs in America have the historical stature of Chicago Golf. Founded in 1895 by the noted player and course architect Charles Blair Macdonald, it was one of five charter members of the United States Golf Association and the home of the first eighteen-hole track in America. The club was also the first in this country to use bentgrass and install

THE CHICAGO GOLF CLUB, THE FIRST EIGHTEEN-HOLE COURSE IN AMERICA, HOSTED ITS FIRST OPEN IN 1897. THAT YEAR JOE LLOYD EDGED OUT FUTURE OPEN GREAT WILLIE ANDERSON BY ONE STROKE, SHOOTING A THREE ON THE 461-YARD FINAL HOLE. CONSIDERING THE DIFFICULTY OF THE HOLE, LLOYD'S THREE ON THE EIGHTEENTH WOULD TODAY BE CONSIDERED A BIRDIE, IF NOT AN EAGLE. AT THE TIME, HOWEVER, NEITHER TERM WAS YET IN USE. (CHICAGO GOLF CLUB)

a watering system. In addition, the club has been the site of three U.S. Opens and four U.S. Amateurs.

The original course at the Wheaton, Illinois, club was designed by Macdonald. The winner of the 1895 U.S. Amateur Championship, he patterned his new track after St. Andrews; pot bunkers, rolling terrain, and grass-covered mounds were all incorporated into the layout.

The U.S. Open first came to the Chicago Golf Club in 1897. In those days the championship was played over only two rounds, and Joe Lloyd won with a two-day total of 162, edging out eighteen-year-old Willie Anderson by a stroke. The clincher for Lloyd was a remarkable three that he carded on the 461-yard eighteenth hole the final day. Macdonald competed in that Open as well and finished tied for eleventh after posting eighty-five and eighty-nine for 174.

Chicago Golf Club was also the venue for the 1900 championship, which saw Harry Vardon make his U.S. Open debut and gain his first and only victory in that event. His four-day score of 313 included an 80 for his last round and would have been lower had the Englishman not whiffed on a tap-in putt at the end of his second eighteen.

Vardon's caddie for the Open that year was Tom Bendelow, who went on to design some four hundred courses across the country, including Medinah No. 3 and the Skokie Country Club (site of the 1922 Open). J.H. Taylor, who ended up two strokes behind Vardon in second

place, enlisted William Marshall as his caddie for the final round; Marshall had started the tournament as a competitor but withdrew after opening with a ninety-one. Macdonald played in this championship as well, but he was never a factor and finished in thirtieth place, forty-two shots behind the winner.

It was another eleven years before the Open returned to Chicago Golf Club. Three men tied for the lead after seventy-two holes, and they met in a play-off the following day. John McDermott shot an eighty and held off Mike Brady and George Simpson to become the first native-born American to win the national championship.

Shortly after hosting their third and final Open, members of the Chicago Golf Club began contemplating a redesign. If the original course had a weakness, many thought, it was that Macdonald penalized a hook and not a slice, which was not that surprising considering that the architect had a tendency to slice the ball himself. So in 1922 they enlisted Seth Raynor, who once worked as Macdonald's chief engineer, to revamp the course. It has hardly changed since.

THE ORIGINAL COURSE AT CHICAGO, DESIGNED BY CHARLES BLAIR MACDONALD, WAS REDESIGNED BY SETH RAYNOR, MACDONALD'S ONETIME CHIEF ENGINEER, IN 1922. (CHICAGO GOLF CLUB)

Colonial Country Club

1941

The Colonial Country Club will forever be known as Ben Hogan's course. It is the home club of the native Texan and his favored practice ground. Built in 1935 by Marvin Leonard, the older of two merchant brothers who operated a discount-style store in Fort Worth, it was one of the first clubs in the South to have bentgrass greens. The course was situated on some 160 acres of land in the southwest part of town, near Forest Park and Texas Christian University and along the Trinity River. When it came time to consider design possibilities, Leonard asked two noted architects, John Bredemus of Texas and Percy Maxwell of Oklahoma, to assist with the layout. Each submitted five alternative plans, and Leonard borrowed elements from each one to create the track that would become Colonial.

Leonard was justifiably proud of the course he had built, and in the late 1930s, he began lobbying the United States Golf Association for the privilege of holding the Open at his new club. That would not be an easy feat, because the national championship had never been played in the South before. But the Colonial founder was persistent, and he finally convinced the folks at the USGA to stage their main event there. But not before they told Leonard that he would have to upgrade holes four and five. Otherwise, they said, they were impressed with the demanding layout he had forged from the pecan trees and hackberry bushes that grew along the Trinity.

Leonard went right to work. He bought some adjoining land and then asked Maxwell and another architect, Dean Woods, to help with the redesign. They did a marvelous job, turning the new acreage into a three-hole stretch that came to be known as the "Horrible Horseshoe." It began with the third hole, a 476-yard dogleg left and the longest par four on a course of long par fours. Next up was the fourth hole, a 246-yard par three, which is followed by a 459-yard, left-to-right dogleg par four that Arnold Palmer once described as "a great hole because, sooner or later, you must play a difficult shot." He went on to say, "I'll take a par there anytime." The alterations added some three hundred yards to the course, making the par seventy, 7,100-yard track a formidable challenge that placed a premium on accurate driving.

A COMPETITOR IN THE 1941 OPEN SHOOTS TO THE FIFTH GREEN. SITUATED ALONG THE BANKS OF THE TRINITY RIVER, THE HOLE IS THE LAST LEG OF THE COURSE'S "HORRIBLE HORSESHOE." (COLONIAL COUNTRY CLUB)

It wasn't long after those changes were incorporated that the U.S. Open came to town. One of the leaders after two rounds was Craig Wood, the Lake Placid, New York, native who had won the Masters just two months before. Naturally, he would have been considered a favorite coming into Colonial, but one morning several weeks before the tournament he hurt his back when he reached over to pick up a razor he had dropped in the bathroom. Wood was forced to play the Open in a heavy leather-and-steel corset as a result, and after taking a double-bogey seven on his first hole, he thought seriously about packing it in. But his playing partner, Tommy Armour, urged him to continue, so he did, carding an opening-round seventy-three and then a seventy-one during a violent storm the next day that left some of the greens and fairways covered with water. Wood shot a pair of seventies over his last two rounds, draining a twenty-foot sidehill putt on the seventy-second hole for his only Open win. Denny Shute finished second, three strokes back, while Johnny Bulla and Ben Hogan tied for third, five shots off the pace.

Colonial has not had another men's national championship, but it was the site of the 1991 U.S. Women's Open, won by Meg Mallon. It also boasts the honor of having hosted a PGA Tour event every year since 1946. The course is still a tough test of golf and remains more or less the same track on which Hogan used to practice so feverishly, although some minor revisions were made in the late 1960s after several holes were damaged by floods.

Columbia Country Club

1921

There wasn't a lot of drama surrounding the 1921 U.S. Open, which was played at the Columbia Country Club in Chevy Chase, Maryland. "Long Jim" Barnes, a lanky Englishman who had already captured two PGA Championships and three Western Opens, fired a first-round sixty-nine and never looked back. Even though he carded a seventy-five on his second eighteen, he still had a four-stroke lead over Fred McLeod, the 1908 Open winner and the Columbia professional, and a five-shot

advantage over nineteen-year-old Bobby Jones. Successive rounds of seventy-three and seventy-two gave Barnes a seventy-two-hole total of 289 and a nine-shot win over McLeod and Walter Hagen. He was so dominant that perhaps the most interesting moment of the tournament occurred as the champion-to-be walked up the eighteenth fairway for the fourth and final time. A Marine band played from behind the green, pausing only long enough for Barnes to putt out, and then president Warren Harding came over to shake his hand. Harding later presented the Open trophy to Barnes, the first and only time the President of the United States has made such a gesture.

It's not surprising that Harding showed up at Columbia, because the club is only a fifteen-minute drive from the White House. Built in 1910, the course was designed by Herbert Barker and set up for the Open as a par seventy, 6,380-yard track. Very little about the course—or the club—has changed since, but that's just the way things seem to work there. It's a quiet spot in the Maryland countryside, steeped in tradition

THE DAUNTING SIXTEENTH HOLE AT COLUMBIA IN CHEVY CHASE, MARYLAND, LOOKS MUCH AS IT DID AT THE TIME OF THE 1921 U.S. OPEN. (USGA)

BRITISH GOLFER JAMES BARNES
DOMINATED THE 1921 OPEN AT
COLUMBIA. AFTER A FIRST-ROUND
SIXTY-NINE, HE FINISHED WITH A NINE-
SHOT LEAD OVER CLUB PROFESSIONAL
FRED MCLEOD. PRESIDENT WARREN
HARDING PRESENTED HIM WITH HIS
TROPHY. (USGA)

and guarded about its privacy. Consider, for example, that between 1913 and 1994 the club had only two head professionals: Fred McLeod held the job for fifty-two years until he retired in 1965 at the age of eighty-three, and then Bill Strausbaugh took over for the next twenty-nine.

Barnes never did contend at another U.S. Open, but four years later he realized a lifelong dream by winning the British Open at historic Prestwick. Barnes had been close before, finishing among the top eight seven times. But on this occasion he finally prevailed, and in doing so became one of only eight players ever to win the U.S. Open, the British Open, and the PGA Championship.

Congressional Country Club

1964, 1997

Mention Congressional Country Club, and the image that comes immediately to mind is that of an exhausted Ken Venturi standing on the thirteenth green one sweltering afternoon in the summer of 1964. His head
is cocked skyward, his eyes are closed, and his face is beaded with
sweat. He has just drained an eighteen-foot birdie putt to boost his lead

THE STATELY CLUBHOUSE AT
CONGRESSIONAL COUNTRY CLUB IS ONE
OF THE LARGEST IN THE WORLD,
CONTAINING AN INDOOR SWIMMING
POOL AND EVEN A BOWLING ALLEY. (USGA)

Congressional Country Club

Host to
64th NATIONAL OPEN
of the
UNITED STATES GOLF ASSOCIATION
18-20 JUNE, 1964

CHAMPIONSHIPS AT CONGRESSIONAL
WERE PLAYED ON A COMPOSITE COURSE
OF THE CLUB'S TWENTY-SEVEN HOLES.
AFTER KEN VENTURI WON HIS ONLY
OPEN IN 1964, HE DECLARED
CONGRESSIONAL THE "BEST COURSE I
EVER WON AN OPEN ON." (USGA)

to three strokes, and for the first time he allows himself to dream that the U.S. Open might actually be his.

But Venturi still has a long way to go. He is light-headed from playing his second round of eighteen on a one-hundred-degree day, and he staggers through the finishing stretch, a doctor following his every move from behind the ropes. He bogeys fourteen but then pars fifteen, sixteen, and seventeen. On the eighteenth he puts his second shot into the right greenside bunker but blasts out to within ten feet of the hole. He studies his putt carefully, and after stroking it into the cup, musters the strength only to drop his club, feebly raise his arms above his head, and mutter: "My God, I've won the Open." His playing partner, Raymond Floyd, picks Venturi's ball from the hole and gives it to the new champ, tears streaming down both their faces. Floyd is only twenty-one years old, but he understands that Venturi has done what most people in golf thought impossible: He has won the national championship even though he hasn't finished first in a tournament in four years, even though he had to qualify for a spot in the '64 Open field, and even though he was six strokes out of the lead at the start of the day.

Venturi's Open victory was one of the most dramatic in history, and Congressional will forever be known as the site of that epic win. But the story of the classy Bethesda, Maryland, club goes back much further than that. It was started in 1924 by two Indiana congressmen—Oscar Bland and O.R. Luhring—who wanted to develop a place near Washington, D.C., where the country's political and business leaders could meet in less formal surroundings. The original eighteen holes were designed by Devereux Emmet, and the founders required that a majority of the board of governors be members of Congress. President Calvin Coolidge offically opened the club, and early members included John D. Rockefeller, Hiram Walker, William Randolph Hearst, Harvey Firestone, and Charlie Chaplin.

As was the case with the rest of the country, Congressional barely survived the Depression. During World War II its huge clubhouse was occupied by the Office of Strategic Services (OSS), which was the fore-runner of the Central Intelligence Agency. The club prospered during

IN 1989, MEMBERS OF CONGRESSIONAL COMMISSIONED REES JONES, SON OF ROBERT TRENT JONES (WHO HAD REMODELED THE COURSE HIMSELF MORE THAN THIRTY YEARS BEFORE), TO REDESIGN THE CLUB'S TWENTY-SEVEN HOLES AND ADD ANOTHER NINE. THE RESULT WAS A CHALLENGING, 7,219-YARD, PAR-SEVENTY-TWO CHAMPIONSHIP COURSE FOR THE OPEN IN 1997. (ROBERT WALKER)

NUMBER TWELVE AT CONGRESSIONAL
OFFERS SEVERAL THREATENING FAIRWAY
BUNKERS, A SIGNIFICANT CHANGE SINCE
DEVEREUX EMMET'S ORIGINAL 1924
DESIGN. (ROBERT WALKER)

the postwar years, however, and members asked Robert Trent Jones to build a new nine in 1957 and revise Emmet's original layout. When the United States Golf Association awarded Congressional the '64 Open, Jones came back and did some more work on the greens. In the late 1980s, the board asked Jones's son Rees to improve upon his father's labors, and after walking the courses several times, he convinced the members to add nine more holes and to almost completely revamp the other twenty-seven. Rees rebuilt every green and put in several mounds and valleys, along with a number of bunkers. The finished product included a tough, par-seventy-two championship course measuring 7,219 yards and a more benign par seventy track of 6,588 yards.

Not surprisingly, Congressional has always been a place for politicians, and several presidents—including Eisenhower, Nixon, Ford, and

Clinton—have played there. But the club has also become a popular spot for families. In addition to the two golf courses, it boasts a bowling alley, three swimming pools, and twenty tennis courts. Once the regular venue for the PGA Tour's Kemper Open, it now hosts only the occasional major championship; the Seniors played their 1995 Open at Congressional, and the U.S. Open will come back in '97.

Englewood Golf Club

1909

At one point in the early 1900s the Englewood Golf Club in northern New Jersey was one of the most popular courses in metropolitan New York. The hilly Donald Ross track was located only a mile from a Hudson River ferry that shuttled people between the Garden State and New York City, giving it easy accessibility. After the George Washington Bridge was built, it became even easier to reach. But the bridge brought as many problems as it did people; it had to be linked to a highway, and that highway had to be built through the center of the golf course.

The Englewood Golf Club disbanded after that, and the two halves of the Ross course that had been bisected by Interstate 80 became

DESIGNED BY DONALD ROSS, THE ENGLEWOOD GOLF CLUB HOSTED THE 1909 OPEN. UNFORTUNATELY, IT DISBANDED AFTER A HIGHWAY WAS BUILT THROUGH THE PROPERTY, AND THE COURSE WAS EVENTUALLY SOLD TO DEVELOPERS. (USGA)

separate public facilities, each having nine holes. One was operated by the city of Leonia and the other by Englewood. Investors bought the Leonia nine in the 1960s, tore up the greens and fairways, and constructed a huge housing development on the grounds. Englewood stayed open and even became a private club again. But when fire destroyed the original clubhouse in 1979, members gave up a second time. The course reverted to public ownership for a short time before being sold to developers.

Thousands of people motor past the old Englewood course every day, but only a few of them know that they are driving over the site of the 1909 U.S. Open. Eighty players entered that tournament, and a relative unknown named David Hunter carded an astounding sixty-eight for the morning round. That made him the first man ever to break seventy in an Open, and considering that seventy-nine was the average score for the 1909 event, he had played a remarkable eighteen holes. Unfortunately, Hunter could not sustain that pace, in the afternoon he flailed his way to an eighty-four.

Tom McNamara played it more steadily, and after shooting seventy-five in the morning, he posted a sub-seventy round all his own (sixty-nine), giving him a thirty-six-hole score of 142 and a four-stroke lead. McNamara was still the man to beat after fifty-four holes, but he began to falter in the afternoon. Perhaps it was the oppressive heat, which had sapped the strength of many of the Open competitors. Or maybe it was the pressure he felt from George Sargent. An Englishman who had served as Harry Vardon's assistant in the United Kingdom, Sargent had started the day five back but had shaved three strokes off of McNamara's lead by the beginning of the afternoon round and two more by the end of the first nine. The two men were tied going into twelve for the final time. But when McNamara bogeyed the hole and Sargent birdied it, the tournament was all but over. Sargent finished strong, ending up with a seventy-one and a four-shot victory.

Sargent never won another major, but he did play a significant role in the development of golf in the United States. He was a charter member of the PGA and president of that organization from 1921 to 1926. He later served as head professional of several fine clubs, including Scioto and Interlachen. Three of his five sons followed him into golf, and one of them, Harold, also went on to become PGA president.

Fresh Meadow Country Club

1932

There was no question about the favorite when the 1932 U.S. Open came to the Fresh Meadow Country Club in Flushing, New York. Not only had Gene Sarazen spent six years working as the head professional at the 6,800-yard A.W. Tillinghast course only a half-hour subway ride from Times Square, but he had also just won the British Open and was playing some of the best golf of his career.

In years past, Sarazen had been a golfer of great daring who built his reputation on taking chances. But he had recently begun to tone down his game and was playing more conservatively. That strategy seemed to have served him well in Great Britain, but it didn't do much for him in New York. He shot seventy-four and seventy-six the first two rounds at Fresh Meadow for a thirty-six-hole score of 150, ten over par and five strokes behind Philip Perkins and Jose Jurado. Things didn't get any better for Sarazen the next morning, and he lost four more strokes to par after only eight holes. Then he hit a high, arcing seven iron to the 143-yard ninth and watched his ball roll to within ten feet. He drained his putt for birdie and headed over to the tenth tee. Bobby Jones was sitting on the clubhouse veranda when Sarazen holed out, and he turned to a friend and said: "This might set Gene off."

AT THE TIME OF THE 1932 U.S. OPEN, FRESH MEADOW WAS ONE OF THE NEW YORK CITY AREA'S MOST POPULAR GOLF COURSES. UNFORTUNATELY, IT NO LONGER EXISTS; FIFTEEN YEARS AFTER GENE SARAZEN'S WIN, THE COURSE WAS SOLD TO DEVELOPERS. (USGA)

It certainly did. Scrapping his uncharacteristically cautious approach, Sarazen started shooting at the pins again. He birdied fourteen, fifteen, and sixteen and carded a thirty-two on the back, giving him a seventy for his morning round. He ate a leisurely lunch with Jones and then went out again in thirty-two. A thirty-four on the back nine gave him a sixty-six and his second U.S. Open title. Sarazen's final-round score was the lowest in history, and his 286 matched the seventy-two-hole record Chick Evans had set at Minikahda in 1916. And by recording a final 36-hole total of 136, he had set a mark that wouldn't be broken for fifty-one years.

The course on which Sarazen shot seventy and sixty-six to win the 1932 Open didn't even exist when Larry Nelson broke the record at Oakmont in 1983. Flushing was in a relatively rural part of the New York City area when Tillinghast built the course, but it had gradually become more urbanized. As that happened, the holders of Fresh Meadow's first mortgage began to put enormous financial pressure on the club. By 1946 the members had had enough, and they decided to buy the nearby Lakeville Club, which had gone bankrupt, and move everything to that location ten miles away. They also agreed to sell the old Tillinghast course to a developer, who later built a shopping center and an apartment complex on the grounds where Gene Sarazen, one of only four men ever to win all four modern majors, played some of the best golf of his life.

Garden City Golf Club

1902

The story of golf in Garden City, New York, began in 1897 when a semi-public, nine-hole course known as The Island Golf Links was built by the Garden City Company, which was in the process of developing a section of Long Island known as the Hempstead Plain. Designed primarily by Devereux Emmet, it used a huge gravel pit as a hazard for two par threes and played over several roads. A second nine was added the following year, and the finished product measured over six thousand

FOUNDED IN 1899, GARDEN CITY HOSTED THE AMATEUR IN 1900 AND THE OPEN TWO YEARS LATER. THE WINNER, LAURIE AUCHTERLONIE, BECAME THE FIRST MAN TO BREAK EIGHTY IN EVERY ROUND OF THE CHAMPIONSHIP. (DAN MCKEAN)

yards. An old farmhouse was used as a locker room, and an Englishman named Fred Rigden charged fifty cents an hour for lessons.

In 1899 the manager of the Garden City Company, George L. Hubbell, suggested that it establish an independent private club centered around the golf course. Other members of upper management agreed, and that spring the Garden City Golf Club was formed. Among the first to join was Charles Blair Macdonald, the great course architect and winner of the inaugural U.S. Amateur, and Walter Travis, a native Australian who would become the finest amateur player of his era.

Garden City quickly developed a reputation as a first-rate course, and in 1900 hosted the U.S. Amateur Championship, which was won by the thirty-nine-year-old Travis. Two years later, Garden City was the site of the U.S. Open. The hot golfer that year was St. Andrews native Laurie Auchterlonie, who became the first man to break eighty in each round of the championship. He finished with a seventy-two-hole score of 307 to win by six strokes. Tied for second were Stewart Gardner and Walter Travis, who had started off with a pair of eighty-twos but then bounced back with seventy-five and seventy-four on the last day. Another strong competitor was noted course architect Donald Ross, who came in ninth, one of four top-ten Open finishes in his playing career.

One reason that Auchterlonie had scored so well at Garden City was the recent introduction of the Haskell rubber-core ball, which flew and ran farther than the old gutta perchas. That concerned club members because they did not want to see new equipment cheapen the challenge of their track so they asked Travis to help them remodel. Bunkers were changed, tees backed up, and greens relocated, all with an eye toward making the layout longer. The par seventy-three course measured nearly 6,800 yards from the championship tees when all work was completed. It still wasn't the longest in the world, but its smallish greens,

DEVEREUX EMMET'S ORIGINAL DESIGN AT GARDEN CITY FEATURED A HUGE GRAVEL PIT AS A HAZARD ON THE PAR-THREE SECOND. THE COURSE WAS REMODELED AND LENGTHENED BY ABOUT EIGHT HUNDRED YARDS BY WILLIAM TRAVIS AFTER THE INTRODUCTION OF THE RUBBER CORE BALL. (USGA)

GARDEN CITY'S SEVERE ROUGH AND EXTENSIVE BUNKERING GIVE IT A GENUINE SCOTTISH-LINKS FEEL, MAKING IT AN EARLY FAVORITE FOR MAJOR COMPETITIONS: FOUR AMATEURS, ONE OPEN, AND THE WALKER CUP.

(DAN McKEAN)

wicked rough, and severe bunkering made it a tough test of skill for all levels of golfers. And it remains that way today. Many members describe it as an old-fashioned course, built in the mode of the great Scottish seaside links with its unique cross-bunkering, hidden fairway hazards, and sloping greens that demand a wide repertoire of shots.

Garden City was the site of several other big events after the U.S. Open; it hosted the U.S. Amateur in 1908, 1913, and 1936 and the Walker Cup in 1924. But it hasn't had a major competition since.

Glen View Club

1904

It was founded in 1897, the brainchild of William Caldwell, a Scotsman and professor of sociology at Northwestern University. He had talked to friends about starting a local golf club, and his ideas were met with such enthusiasm that a committee was quickly formed to determine whether that was possible. It was, and less than a year later the Glen View Club of Golf, Illinois, was born. Founding members paid a one-hundred dollar initiation fee, and annual dues were set at fifty dollars. The club was located on a 180-acre tract that had been purchased from the Dewes family, who had homesteaded the land in the 1840s. Members often came up from Chicago by train and were met at the station by carriage or horse-drawn bus. In 1906, a group of men started the North Shore and Western Railway, which ran between North Evanston and the club and was used to haul caddies, employees, and members to and from the grounds. The rail company operated until 1926, when it was sold; most members at that point were driving their own cars to the club and no longer needed the train.

EARLY MEMBERS OF THE GLEN VIEW CLUB, WHICH WAS BUILT BY HERBERT JAMES TWEEDIE IN 1897, OFTEN CAME IN FROM CHICAGO BY TRAIN TO BE MET AT THE STATION BY A HORSE-DRAWN CARRIAGE THAT TOOK THEM TO THE REMOTE CLUB. THE CARRIAGE ROAD CUT ACROSS THE FAIRWAY ON THE EIGHTEENTH. (GLEN VIEW CLUB)

The original course was a par eighty-three, 6,051-yard layout designed by Richard Leslie, who also served as the club's first professional and groundskeeper. In 1899 it was the site of the first Western Open, and in 1902 the U.S. Amateur was held there. But the biggest golfing event ever to take place at Glen View was the 1904 U.S. Open. Willie Anderson was the defending champion, and he started the two-day, seventy-two-hole tourney with an opening round of seventy-five. He shot a seventy-eight that afternoon and turned in the same score the following morning. And then Anderson caught on fire, scorching the Glen View course with a seventy-two, at that time the lowest round in Open history. He finished five strokes ahead of his nearest competitor and took home two-hundred dollars for his win.

The Glen View course has changed over the years, most significantly in 1922 when William Flynn was asked to revamp the track. A noted architect who also designed Cherry Hills in Denver and is credited with

GLEN VIEW HAS CHANGED SIGNIFICANTLY SINCE WILLIE ANDERSON'S OPEN WIN THERE IN 1904. MOST NOTABLE WAS WILLIAM FLYNN'S 1922 REMODEL, WHEN HE INCREASED THE COURSE'S YARDAGE TO 6,362 AND DROPPED PAR TO SEVENTY-TWO. (GLEN VIEW CLUB)

updating the venerable Shinnecock Hills course, Flynn added yardage, turned hole seventeen into a dogleg par four with an elevated green, modified a number of the other holes and dropped par to seventy-two. Today, the course plays 6,362 yards, and par remains the same.

From the beginning, Glen View has enjoyed a reputation as one of the finest golf clubs in the country. Author Joseph E. Ryan wrote about the course in a 1903 book on sports: "From a picturesque standpoint, Glen View is without peer in the Western golfing world. Practically hewn out of primeval forest, its contour shows pleasing evidence of the landscape-gardener's art. While the distances were not designed with a view to intensify the scenic effect, the course looks like a well-laid-out park."

Almost as well regarded as the course itself is the man who served as head professional there from 1918 to 1953, Jock Hutchison. A St. Andrews native and one of the top golfers of his time, Hutchison won the Western Open twice, the British Open once, the PGA Championship once, and was runner-up in two U.S. Opens. Born two years before Glen View was founded, he died in 1977.

Hazeltine National Golf Club

1970, 1991

The Hazeltine National Golf Club was founded in 1962 with one purpose and one purpose only. And that, according to the club's original mission statement, was to host national championships. Conceived by Totton P. Heffelfinger and designed by Robert Trent Jones, it was situated on a beautiful stretch of rolling farmland outside Minneapolis. Initially, some of the investors wanted to call it The Executive Golf Club of Minnesota and hoped it would be part of a network of similarly named clubs around the country with reciprocal privileges for the members. But that moniker turned off most locals, and so the club was named Hazeltine, after the vast lake that bordered a section of the property.

Jones built two courses there. One was a championship track of 7,151 yards that featured several sharp doglegs and a number of blind

FOUNDED IN 1962, HAZELTINE ROLLS
ACROSS THE PICTURESQUE COUNTRYSIDE
OUTSIDE OF MINNEAPOLIS. (RICHARD
HAMILTON SMITH)

shots and the other a nine-hole children's layout. A former president of the United States Golf Association, Heffelfinger began lobbying his colleagues at the organization for an event right away. They gave him the 1966 Women's Open, and when that came off without a hitch, they decided to hold the men's championship at his club four years later.

It was, by most accounts, a disaster. Winds blew as hard as forty knots, and the average first-round score was seventy-nine. But the real problem, most pros thought, was the course. Jack Nicklaus said Hazeltine lacked definition and added, "The only target on the tee at eighteen was the chimney on Tot Heffelfinger's house"; Bob Rosburg commented, "Jones has so many doglegs on this course that he must have laid it out in a kennel"; and William Hyndman exclaimed, "I feel like I've just been in a fistfight!" But the most acerbic comments came from Dave Hill. When asked what Hazeltine lacked, he replied: "Eighty acres of corn and a few cows. They ruined a good farm when they built this course." Hill made headlines when his remarks were reported in the papers the following day, and members of the gallery mooed whenever he walked by.

Unfortunately, all that criticism obscured some terrific play by Tony Jacklin, who posted three seventies and a seventy-one to win by seven strokes and become the first Englishman to capture a U.S. Open title in fifty years. The runner-up? Dave Hill, of all people. And was it purely coincidence that the fifteen-thousand dollar second-place check he received a few days later was not signed?

It seemed unlikely that Hazeltine would ever get another shot at a U.S. Open, even after the club made significant changes to the course. But it did win the right to host the 1983 U.S. Senior Open, and that went so well that the USGA decided to give it a second chance.

Hazeltine had five years to prepare for the 1991 championship, and even though it had already revamped the old course, it was leaving nothing to chance. The club brought in Rees Jones, son of the original architect, to work on the track. The result was a wonderful par seventy-two of 7,149 yards with four par fives ranging from 518 yards to 590 yards, four par threes of varying lengths and five par fours that measured more than 430 yards.

The players loved the new course, and even Dave Hill commented on how much the club had improved upon the original. Payne Stewart fired an opening-round sixty-seven and held the lead for the first three days. But he struggled on Sunday and was two down to his playing partner Scott Simpson after fifteen. Simpson bogeyed sixteen, however, bringing Stewart a stroke closer, and when he did the same on eighteen, they were tied. They met the following day in a playoff, and the match unfolded in a familiar fashion. Simpson again stood on the sixteenth tee

REES JONES ADDED SOME CHARACTER TO HIS FATHER'S ORIGINAL LAYOUT, BUT KEPT IT TOUGH WITH ITS SHARP DOGLEGS AND BLIND SHOTS. (RICHARD HAMILTON SMITH)

with a two-stroke lead, but he proceeded to bogey the last three holes. Stewart, on the other hand, birdied sixteen, and after parring seventeen and eighteen ended up with a two-stroke win and his second major championship.

Hazeltine has not been awarded another Open yet, but given the way it held up during the 1991 event, it almost certainly will get the nod again. And why shouldn't it? After all, this is a club that was made to host national championships.

Interlachen Country Club

1930

The Interlachen Country Club got its start in 1909 when a group of six men purchased 146 acres of farmland on the outskirts of Minneapolis. Their plan was to build a golf course, and according to local legend, the group sent two of its members—G.B. Bickelhaupt and Ransom Powell—out to the property to close the sale. The men brought twelve-thousand dollars in gold bullion and certificates, but the farmer who owned the land refused to keep that much money in his house. So the buyers

WHEN BOBBY JONES WON THE 1930 OPEN AT INTERLACHEN, HE WAS ONLY ONE VICTORY AWAY FROM THE COVETED GRAND SLAM; HE COMPLETED THAT REMARKABLE FEAT TEN WEEKS LATER WHEN HE TOOK THE U.S. AMATEUR AT MERION. (PAUL HAMILTON)

INTERLACHEN'S SEVENTH HOLE IS A
SHORT PAR FOUR. ORIGINALLY DESIGNED
BY WILLIE WATSON IN 1910, THE
COURSE HAS CHANGED VERY LITTLE
SINCE DONALD ROSS'S REMODEL IN 1919.

(RICHARD HAMILTON SMITH)

returned to the city and guarded their hoard all night with a loaded shotgun, waiting for the banks to open the following morning. Only then were they able to seal the deal.

The club was incorporated on New Year's Eve 1909 and officially opened in late July two years later. The original course was designed by Willie Watson, but Donald Ross remodeled the entire track in 1919. And, if he returned today, he would have no trouble recognizing the 6,721-yard, par-seventy-two layout. To be sure, there have been some changes over the years: former club professional Willie Kidd converted the old sixteenth into a short par four and built a new tee for the par-three seventeenth, while Robert Trent Jones modified the first and third holes, and Geoffrey Cornish installed new bunkers on six holes (two, three, four, five, six, and fourteen) and relocated traps on seven, ten, and eleven. Still, Interlachen remains a classic Ross creation, a beautifully wooded track on gentle rolling land that has been ranked among America's top one hundred courses by *Golf Digest* ever since the magazine began the ratings in 1966.

Interlachen has hosted only one U.S. Open, but it was among the best. The year was 1930, and the player to watch was Bobby Jones. He had been in England earlier that summer, and after helping the U.S. team win the Walker Cup, he had captured both the British Amateur and British Open titles. Upon his return to New York, Jones was greeted with a ticker-tape parade up Broadway and then feted at a sumptuous dinner party for four hundred people. The next day he boarded the Twentieth Century Limited for Interlachen and the third leg of golf's Grand Slam.

It was brutally hot that first day, and Jones sweated so profusely that his red foulard tie ran and stained his white shirt. But he managed to post a seventy-one, leaving him just one shot off the lead. He carded a seventy-three for his second eighteen and a sixty-eight for his third, putting him ahead by five strokes. Jones struggled during his final round. He shot thrity-eight on the front and after a double bogey at thirteen had only a one-stroke lead. Birdies at fourteen and sixteen put him back up by three, but he pushed his drive badly on the monster-ous (262-yard) 17th and lost his ball after it hit a tree and seemed to have disappeared into a dried-up swamp. Jones wasn't sure exactly where his ball had gone, and he asked the referee, a Connecticut man named Prescott Bush (whose young son George would become president one day), for a ruling. Bush thought the ball had indeed gone into the mire and allowed the golfer to take what some felt was a liberal penalty drop in the fairway. Jones recorded a double-bogey five on the hole, and after

DONALD ROSS REDESIGNED INTERLACHEN'S FAIRWAYS, LIKE THIS ONE ON THE PAR-THREE THIRD, TO FAVOR ACCURACY OF SHOTS MORE THAN LENGTH. THE ROLLING SLOPES WILL OFTEN KICK OFF-LINE SHOTS INTO STRATEGICALLY PLACED HAZARDS. (RICHARD HAMILTON SMITH)

birdieing eighteen, finished his last loop with a seventy-five, giving him a seventy-two-hole score of 287 and a two-shot win over Macdonald Smith. Ten weeks later in the U.S. Amateur at Merion, Jones completed his remarkable Slam. Shortly thereafter, he retired.

The 1935 Women's Amateur was held at Interlachen, as was the 1986 Senior Amateur Championship and the 1993 Walker Cup, which was won by the U.S. team. The club was slated to be the venue for the 1942 Open, but the tournament was canceled due to World War II. That was probably Interlachen's last chance to host another national championship, because although it certainly had the course, it didn't have the facilities to handle the massive crowds that had begun gathering for the event each year.

Inverness Club

1920, 1931, 1957, 1979

Inverness came into being in 1903 when a nine-hole course was built on a section of land in Toledo, Ohio by a man named Bernard Nichols. Fifteen years later the members upgraded, and after acquiring some neighboring property, hired Donald Ross to construct an eighteen-hole track. Ross revamped Nichols's original half-course and added nine holes of his own. Shortly after that work was completed, the club hosted the 1919 Ohio State Open, and the reviews of the new course were so positive that the United States Golf Association decided to bring the U.S. Open there the following year.

The 1920 championship is remembered as being the first Open for Bobby Jones, Gene Sarazen, Tommy Armour, and Johnny Farrell, a foursome who would go on to win eight national titles among them. But perhaps it is even better known as the last time the great but aging English pair, Harry Vardon and Ted Ray, played in a U.S. Open. And what a farewell it was. Vardon, who was fifty years old, shocked the golfing world by taking the lead after fifty-four holes, one ahead of Jock Hutchison and Leo Diegel and two up on Ray. But he faltered during the afternoon round when a windstorm blew up off Lake Erie and could

manage only a seventy-eight for a seventy-two-hole score of 296. Not to worry, for his good friend Ray, who was forty-three, played the front one under par. Wearing his trademark felt fedora and puffing on his briar pipe, he struggled on the back to a forty but made his par on eighteen for a seventy-five, giving him a total of 295 and his only Open win.

The championship returned to Inverness in 1931, but it was played on a somewhat different course. As good as Ross's design was, the introduction of steel-shafted clubs had weakened it a bit, so the members asked A.W. Tillinghast to make their layout tougher. A former resident of Toledo, Tillinghast designed four new greens, added several bunkers, lengthened the course by some three hundred yards and lowered par one stroke to seventy-one.

The Open that year was a tournament of extremes. The temperatures on the opening day soared over a hundred degrees, and the weather remained brutally hot throughout the weekend. It also took forever to determine a winner. After Billy Burke and George Von Elm finished even after seventy-two holes, they met in a thirty-six-hole play-off. But they both shot 149 and had to face off again the following day, with Burke winning by one. It was a terrific battle that went back

THE SECOND GREEN AT INVERNESS WAS DESIGNED BY DONALD ROSS IN 1919. THE COURSE HAS UNDERGONE FOUR REMODELS SINCE EDWARD RAY PLAYED THIS HOLE ON THE WAY TO HIS 1920 OPEN VICTORY. (USGA)

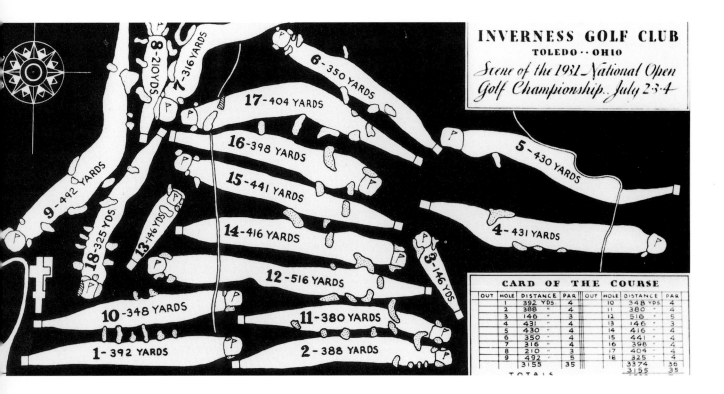

A SCORECARD ILLUSTRATES THE LAYOUT AT INVERNESS AT THE TIME OF THE 1931 OPEN. AFTER BILLY BURKE AND GEORGE VON ELM BATTLED THROUGH TWO EXHAUSTING THIRTY-SIX-HOLE PLAY-OFFS, THE USGA RESTRICTED PLAY-OFFS TO EIGHTEEN HOLES WITH SUDDEN DEATH IN THE EVENT OF A TIE. (USGA)

and forth over 144 holes, and when it was over, Burke became known as the only man who had to play two Opens to win one.

Inverness didn't get the Open back again until 1957, but the membership didn't seem to mind the wait. In fact, they even spruced up the course again. The architect this time was Dick Wilson, and he rebuilt ten of the tees, added several bunkers, changed the ninth from a par five to a par four, and extended the track more than four hundred yards. Jimmy Demaret seemed to like the alterations. The forty-seven-year-old grandfather carded an opening-round sixty-eight and led the pack at the end of fifty-four holes by a stroke. He shot a solid seventy-two on Saturday afternoon but finished one stroke back of Dick Mayer and Cary Middlecoff, who met the following day in a play-off that Mayer won. The course was not so kind to a seventeen-year-old rookie named Jack Nicklaus, who missed the cut after going eighty and eighty. But he would do better in years to come.

Inverness hosted a fourth Open in 1979, and the pretournament primping was handled by George and Tom Fazio, who spent most of their time building four new holes. Hale Irwin won the championship in rather undramatic fashion; he had a six-stroke lead heading into the back nine on Sunday and then proceeded to shoot a five-over forty. "I started choking on the first tee," Irwin said afterward. "This was not your casual round of Sunday golf." But he was never seriously challenged that day, and even though he carded a seventy-five, he was still good enough to beat Jerry Pate and Gary Player by two shots for his second Open title.

Lon Hinkle didn't even come close to contending in '79. He finished tied for fifty-third after shooting eighty-one on Sunday, but his name will always be associated with that event because of a drive he made the first day on the eighth hole. Rather than hitting his ball down the fairway of the dogleg left, Hinkle cranked a one iron between a pair of oak trees to the left of the tee and onto the seventeenth fairway. From there he hit a three iron to the eighth green and two-putted for his birdie. Five other players used that same approach that day, but when they walked

THE CREEK THAT WINDS ACROSS THE FAIRWAY AND ALONG ITS RIGHT SIDE MAKES ACCURACY ESSENTIAL ON THE PAR-FOUR SEVENTH, A DOGLEG LEFT. WITH THE CHARACTERISTIC DONALD ROSS ELEVATED GREEN TO CONTEND WITH AS WELL, GOLFERS REGULARLY TURN IN DOUBLE BOGEYS ON THE HOLE. (USGA)

to the eighth tee the following morning, they found the USGA had
planted a huge spruce in the gap between the two oaks to eliminate the
shortcut and force the contestants to play the hole as it had been
designed. The spruce still stands, and it has always been known as
Hinkle's Tree.

Inwood Country Club

1923

It was the year 1900 when tobacco merchant Jacob Wertheim fell in love with Emma Stern and asked her to be his wife. The avid golfer who hailed from Far Rockaway, New York, said yes, and the two set a date to be married. As they prepared for that day, Wertheim began to think of special things he could do for his lovely bride-to-be, and it wasn't long before he decided to build her a golf course. Emma Stern, it seems, had no place to play the game she loved so much. To remedy that, Wertheim rented a potato farm in the Long Island town of Inwood and hired two men—Dr. William Exton and Arthur Thatcher—to lay out a nine-hole course on the grounds. And so Inwood Country Club was

GOLF LEGEND BOBBY JONES TEES OFF AT THE 1923 OPEN AT INWOOD. THE COURSE HAS NOT BEEN ALTERED SINCE THE TIME OF JONES'S FIRST OPEN VICTORY, SO PLAYERS TODAY BATTLE MANY OF THE SAME OBSTACLES— INCLUDING THE CREEK ON THE EIGHTEENTH CRUCIALLY CARRIED BY JONES FOR HIS WIN. (EDWIN LEVICK, COURTESY USGA)

BOBBY JONES, POISED TO WIN AT THE EIGHTEENTH IN THE FINAL ROUND OF THE 1923 OPEN, DOUBLE-BOGEYED FOR A TIE WITH BOBBY CRUIKSHANK. STILL TIED ON THE SEVENTEENTH IN THE PLAY-OFF THE NEXT DAY, IT WAS CRUIKSHANK'S TURN TO DOUBLE-BOGEY. JONES PUTTS HERE ON THE EIGHTEENTH FOR PAR AND HIS FIRST MAJOR CHAMPIONSHIP. (G. PIETZCKER, COURTESY USGA)

born. The first club professional was a Scotsman named William Martin, and Wertheim paid him an annual salary of two-hundred dollars. But Martin left after the first season because he could make more money working as a taxi driver.

The next Inwood professional was Edward Eriksen, a former baseball player who knew next to nothing about golf. But he was a good athlete who caught on quickly and eventually became a well-regarded player and pro. He also dabbled in design and, in 1906, built another nine holes at the club. Ten years later, one of Eriksen's successors, Herbert Strong, rebuilt and modernized the entire course. He did such a good job on the links-style track located just a mile from the Atlantic Ocean that Inwood was selected shortly thereafter as the site of the 1921 PGA Championship. And two years later the club hosted the U.S. Open.

It was an exciting competition. Twenty-one-year-old Bobby Jones led the field after fifty-four holes and was paired with Gene Sarazen for the final round. Jones shot a thirty-nine on the front and played the first six holes on the back side in two under par. But he bogeyed sixteen and seventeen and doubled eighteen to end the day with a seventy-six. He was upset at the way he had staggered home, but it still looked like he would prevail, especially after his closest competitor, Bobby Cruickshank, double-bogeyed the sixteenth. But the Englishman bounced back and forced a play-off after draining a five-foot putt on the seventy-second hole.

Jones appeared a bit shaken when he showed up the next day, and given how he had finished the afternoon before, it was easy to understand why. Although he was considered to be among the finest players

INWOOD'S COURSE IS SITUATED ALONG JAMAICA BAY ON LONG ISLAND. LIBERAL BUNKERING AND ITS SEASIDE FEEL COMPLETE THE EFFECT OF THIS LINKS-STYLE TRACK. (USGA)

of that time, he had yet to win a major championship, and the Georgia native was beginning to doubt himself. Carding that miserable double on eighteen didn't help. But Jones settled down in time to par the first hole, and the match was on. The two men fought gallantly that afternoon, and they were tied as they stood on the eighteenth tee. Both put their drives into the rough, and neither seemed capable of carrying a pond that guarded the green with their second shots. Cruickshank played it safe and laid up. But Jones reached into his bag for a three iron and, in what is regarded as one of the greatest shots in Open history, smacked his approach to within six feet of the pin. He two-putted for a four to beat Cruickshank, who went on to card a six, by two strokes and capture the first of his thirteen major titles.

Inwood hasn't had another big tournament since, but the 6,647-yard, par-72 course is still a highly regarded layout that has changed little since the day Bobby Jones hit that remarkable shot.

Medinah Country Club

1949, 1975, 1990

Twenty miles from Lake Michigan in the northern Illinois town of Medinah rises an extraordinary mosque-like structure sixty thousand square feet in size. Its design is mostly Byzantine, although it also has elements of Italian, Oriental, and Louis XIV styles. The building features a sixty-foot-high rotunda inlaid with mosaics and a ballroom with a beautifully frescoed ceiling. It took four years—and $600,000—to build, and when it was completed, it became the centerpiece of the Medinah Country Club, one of the finest in the land.

Conceived as a place for men of the Ancient Order of Nobles of the Mystic Shrine and their families, Medinah opened for business in 1925.

THE SECOND HOLE ON MEDINAH'S NO. 3 COURSE IS A PAR THREE OF ONLY 183 YARDS, BUT A WATER HAZARD IN FRONT OF THE GREEN SWALLOWS SHORT DRIVES. AT THE 1975 OPEN, PAT FITZSIMMONS ACED THE HOLE WITH A SIX-IRON ONLY FORTY MINUTES AFTER TEEING OFF— THE QUICKEST ACE IN OPEN HISTORY.
(ROBERT WALKER)

Each of the club's fifteen-hundred charter members paid an initiation fee of one thousand dollars, and in keeping with the spirit of the Roaring Twenties, they used that money to create a wildly extravagant center for sports and recreation. They built a swimming pool, a skating rink, skeet and trap fields, a ski jump, a polo field and an archery range. They also began laying out golf courses. The first one was completed by the time the club formally opened and a second track shortly thereafter. A third, intended for the wives and daughters of club members, was designed by one of the Shriners himself, a Scottish immigrant named Tom Bendelow; it was finished in 1928. But the 6,215-yard, par seventy-one course was deemed too difficult for the women of the Windy City and was closed down a few months after it had opened. Going back to the drawing board, the club decided to create a different sort of course on the same site, one that could be used for championship events. The new track was a par seventy and came out forty-six yards shorter than the original. But it wasn't as difficult as the designers had hoped, and the local pros tore it up in the 1930 Medinah Open. So the club fathers decided to try again. This time they had Englishman Harry Collis help create seven new holes, remodel two others, and add nearly six hundred yards. It reopened in 1934 and fifteen years later was the site of the U.S. Open.

THE GREEN ON MEDINAH'S THIRTEENTH HOLE IS PROTECTED BY A FORTRESS OF WATER AND SAND. (ROBERT WALKER)

With Ben Hogan out of action as a result of his near-fatal car accident, Sam Snead was the pretournament favorite. But after three rounds he trailed Cary Middlecoff, the young Memphis dentist, by six strokes. Alas, Middlecoff struggled during the final round, carding a seventy-five for a seventy-two-hole total of 286. Perhaps sensing that the U.S. Open trophy might finally be his, Snead caught fire on the back nine and needed only to par the last two holes to win. Unfortunately, he posted a bogey four at seventeen and came up short again.

By the time the Open returned to Medinah in 1975, the course had undergone several changes: par had been raised to seventy-one, and the track measured 7,032 yards. An impressive group of players gathered for the event, but most of them faltered, leaving Lou Graham and John Mahaffey to battle each other to a tie after seventy-two holes and then meet in a play-off. Graham shot a seventy-one to Mahaffey's seventy-three to win the only major of his career.

For a while it seemed that would be the last Open at Medinah because the United States Golf Association felt the number 3 course had many weaknesses. Most of that criticism swirled around the eighteenth hole; officials thought the dogleg bent too soon, and there wasn't enough seating around the green for spectators. Anxious to attract another major, the club brought in architect Roger Packard, and he ripped up much of the back nine. Not surprisingly, the biggest changes were to eighteen, which became a 440-yard par four with gallery seating for five thousand. After work was completed, the course had a par of seventy-two, a maximum length of 7,667 yards, and plenty of long, tight holes.

The USGA liked the changes so much that it brought the Open back to Medinah in 1990. It was a stirring event, thanks mostly to Hale Irwin, who drained a forty-five-foot putt on the seventy-second hole to earn the right to meet journeyman Mike Donald in a play-off the next day. "I'll never forget that putt," says Irwin, who sprinted around the green high-fiving fans after his ball had dropped. "It didn't win the Open, but it certainly put me into a position to do so. I also remember how well I hit the ball that afternoon, playing the last eight holes five under par."

The Joplin, Missouri, native met Donald the following day in an eighteen-hole play-off. "I was three down with two to play," Irwin recalls. "But I birdied sixteen, and Mike bogeyed. Then I birdied seventeen to close the gap to one. And then we were tied after Mike bogeyed eighteen, and I parred." The two went into sudden death, and Donald's death could not have been more sudden because Irwin stroked a ten-foot birdie putt on the first green to capture his third Open title.

Merion Golf Club

1934, 1950, 1971, 1981

Merion got its start at the end of the Civil War, but it was cricket, not golf, that brought a group of Philadelphians together to found the club. Its primary focus remained cricket for the next thirty years, but as golf became more and more popular, the members decided to buy one hundred acres of nearby land and build their own layout. A crude nine-hole track was quickly constructed and soon after expanded to eighteen holes. Known as the Haverford Course, it was good enough to host the 1904 and 1909 Women's Amateurs. But advances in golf equipment began to make it—and other tracks around the country—nearly obsolete. So club members started nosing around for another piece of property on which it could build an even bigger and better course.

Eventually, the members settled on an abandoned farm in the nearby town of Ardmore, and a five-man committee was formed to oversee design and construction of a new layout. Its chairman was Hugh Wilson, an insurance broker who had a passion for the game but absolutely no training in course architecture. The committee sent him

COURSE ARCHITECT HUGH WILSON GOT THE IDEA FOR TOPPING MERION'S FLAG POLES WITH WICKER BASKETS FROM A COURSE HE VISITED ON A TRIP TO BRITAIN. THEY HAVE BEEN A TRADEMARK AT MERION EVER SINCE.
(ROBERT WALKER)

THE COURSE AT MERION HAS CHANGED
VERY LITTLE SINCE PERRY MAXWELL
REMODELED THE GREENS IN 1939. THE
PAR-FOUR FIFTH PRESENTS MANY OF THE
SAME CHALLENGES FACED BY BEN
HOGAN IN HIS 1950 OPEN VICTORY.
(ROBERT WALKER)

to England and Scotland to study the great courses, and when he returned, the club started construction. Merion East was completed in 1912, and a shorter West track was added two years later. Perhaps their most interesting features were the wicker baskets that sat on top of the flagsticks. Wilson had found that many of the courses on the other side of the Atlantic didn't have flags on their pins because they were constantly being shredded by strong winds. Some clubs, for example, used small lobster pots instead. But Wilson's favorites were the wicker baskets at the Sunningdale Golf Club outside London, and he thought they would look good at Merion.

Wilson died in 1925, and shortly afterward architect William Flynn came in to do some remodeling. The club hired Percy Maxwell in 1939 to revamp the greens, but otherwise it has done little with the course since the early days. The championship layout at Merion East has often been criticized as being too short for the pros. Given that it measures only 6,500 yards, there is some validity to that argument. But Merion has always played tougher than it looks. After competing in the 1934 Open, Walter Hagen is reported to have said, "This is the type of course where you feel after every round that you can break seventy your next round. But you don't." It is a tight track that puts a premium on accuracy and control, not on raw power. And it is simply one of the top courses around. Jack Nicklaus once said, "Acre for acre, it may be the best test of golf in the world." When Dan Jenkins selected *Sports Illustrated*'s Best 18 Holes in America, Merion was the only club that had two on the list.

Good as the course may be in terms of design, style, and elegance, it also holds a hallowed spot in most golfers' hearts because some of the game's greatest moments have unfolded on its fairways and greens. And a few of those moments have occurred during Merion's four U.S. Opens.

The club held its first national championship in 1934, and the story of that tournament was Olin Dutra roaring back from eight shots down to win with 293. Dutra, who was suffering from a case of amoebic

THE MERION GOLF CLUB HAS AN ILLUSTRIOUS HISTORY. IT BEGAN LIFE AS THE MERION CRICKET CLUB DURING THE CIVIL WAR. A GOLF COURSE WAS ADDED IN 1896, BUT THE PRESENT COURSE WASN'T BUILT UNTIL 1908. (HENRY MILLER)

dysentery at the time, edged Gene Sarazen, who had held the lead after fifty-four holes but then staggered to a seventy-eight the last round. His Waterloo was the famed eleventh hole, where Bobby Jones had completed his Grand Slam four years before. Sarazen had the lead at the tee, but he opted to hit his drive with an iron, not a wood, and hooked it into the Baffling Brook. After taking a drop, he knocked his third shot into a bunker and ended up with a triple-bogey seven.

The championship returned to Merion in 1950; it will forever be known as Ben Hogan's Open. It had been only sixteen months since the Hawk was nearly killed in an automobile accident, and he had to wrap his legs in bandages each day before going onto the course. He was in great pain by the end of the tourney and could barely stand at times. His caddie picked his ball out of the holes for him, and his playing partner the final day, Cary Middlecoff, marked his balls. Hogan finished tied after seventy-two holes with Lloyd Mangrum and George Fazio, and there was some doubt whether he would be able to make the play-off. But the Hawk summoned up the strength not only to walk another eighteen holes but also to shoot a stunning sixty-nine and win the title.

Twenty-one years later, a play-off again decided the Open at Merion. This one was between Lee Trevino and Jack Nicklaus, the two best players of the time. They had tied Sunday at 280, and as they waited on the first tee to go off the following day, Trevino reached into his bag and tossed a rubber snake at Nicklaus. A woman spectator shrieked in fright, but the Golden Bear burst out laughing. The players turned deadly serious when the match started, however, and Trevino was up by one after nine. He shot thrity-two on the back to Nicklaus's thirty-four, giving him a sixty-eight and his second Open title in four years.

Merion's last Open came in 1981, and that championship belonged to Australian David Graham. Graham hovered just off the lead the entire tournament, making his move on Sunday with a brilliant sixty-seven that gave him a three-shot win over Bill Rogers. His seventy-two-hole total of 273 was seven strokes under par and only one shot off the Open record set a year earlier at Baltusrol by Jack Nicklaus, giving further credence to the argument that the grand course of Ardmore just wasn't up to the task anymore.

Merion hasn't hosted another Open since '81, and it probably never will. In addition to being too short, it lacks sufficient parking space as well as facilities for corporate entertaining. But even if it has fallen out of the Open rotation, it remains, as Jack Nicklaus said, one of the best courses in the world.

Midlothian Country Club

1914

The club opened in 1898, and the founding members named it Midlothian after Sir Walter Scott's book of poems, *The Heart of Midlothian*. Their primary interest was golf, and they asked Herbert J. Tweedie to build a pair of courses on some land outside the Illinois town of Blue Island. One was an eighteen-hole championship track measuring a shade over 6,300 yards, and the other a nine-hole layout known as the qualifier because members had to play it with reasonable prowess before they would be allowed on the bigger course. The founders spared little

expense in constructing their courses, even importing sod from Scotland for the fairways. The finished product was quickly regarded as one of the best layouts in the United States, and in 1901 it hosted the Western Open. Six years later Midlothian was the site of the Women's Amateur, and in 1914 the U.S. Open came to town.

Sixty-six golfers started the first day of the Open, and it's safe to say that none of them was feeling as badly as Walter Hagen. Only twenty-one years old at the time, the high-living Rochester, New York, native had gone out for a big lobster dinner the night before. But apparently the food did not set well with him, and he awoke in the middle of the night with severe stomach pains. Hagen could barely stand in the morning, but he forced himself to go out to the course. He claimed he felt pain in every swing, but somehow managed to shoot an opening-round sixty-eight. Hagen wasn't nearly as thrilled with the two-over-par seventy-four he turned in that afternoon, but he still ended the day in first place, with a one-stroke lead over Tom McNamara.

Hagen laid off the seafood that night and ate steak and potatoes instead. He said he felt fine the next morning, but he didn't play like it and could do no better than seventy-five. Fortunately for him, the rest of the field was struggling as well, and Hagen actually increased his lead by another stroke. McNamara collapsed in the final round, but the amateur Chick Evans suddenly heated up and shot seventy. He almost carded a sixty-nine, but he missed a gallant try for eagle after driving his ball to the edge of the eighteenth green. Hagen witnessed this from

ALTHOUGH MOST HOLES AT MIDLOTHIAN APPEAR TO BE SIMPLE AND STRAIGHTFORWARD, STRATEGICALLY PLACED WATER HAZARDS SCATTERED ABOUT THE COURSE ADD A SIGNIFICANT CHALLENGE. (PAT SEELIG)

WALTER HAGEN BECAME THE FIRST EVER
TO BREAK SEVENTY IN A U.S. OPEN
WITH A FIRST-ROUND 68 AT THE 1914
OPEN AT MIDLOTHIAN. HAGEN WENT
ON TO WIN THE TOURNAMENT DESPITE A
BOUT WITH FOOD POISONING THE NIGHT
BEFORE. (PAT SEELIG)

the gallery, and when the shot did not fall, he became the champion. Locked in a tie for third, seven strokes back, were Fred McLeod, who had served at one time as the Midlothian head professional, and George Sargent. It was Hagen's first major, and he would go on to win many more, including another U.S. Open (1919), five PGA Championships, and four British Opens.

Midlothian has hosted a handful of other big tournaments over the years, including the 1907 Women's Amateur and the 1969 and 1973 Western Opens. It once was a popular spot for fox hunting and polo as well, and the club had so many sporting events for its members that a resident jeweler was employed to keep the engravings on the various cups and trophies up to date.

Minikahda Club

1916

Charles Evans, Jr., better known as Chick, was considered one of the top amateur players in the country when he arrived at the Minikahda Club in Minneapolis for the 1916 U.S. Open. A former caddie from the Chicago area, he had won the city amateur championship in 1907 when he was seventeen years old, and two years later captured the first of eight Western Amateur titles. In 1910 he won the Western Open, and he came in second at the 1914 U.S. Open at the Midlothian Country Club, only one stroke back of Walter Hagen. He had also done well in the U.S. Amateur, reaching the semifinals four times and the finals once.

Not surprisingly, many observers pegged Evans as one of the favorites at Minikahda. Chick quickly showed that he was worthy of their support by playing the first nine in thirty-two. Carrying only

UNFORTUNATELY, THE OPEN FIELDS AND VIEW OF LAKE CALHOUN THAT SURROUNDED MINIKAHDA AT THE TIME OF CHARLES EVANS'S 1916 OPEN VICTORY HAVE BEEN REPLACED BY A VIEW OF HOUSING DEVELOPMENTS. (USGA)

Golf Courses of the U.S. Open

CHICK EVANS, WHO ALSO WON THE AMATEUR THE YEAR OF HIS 1916 OPEN VICTORY AT MINIKAHDA, SET A SEVENTY-TWO-HOLE RECORD OF 286 AT THE OPEN THAT HELD FOR MORE THAN TWENTY YEARS. (PAT SEELIG)

seven hickory-shafted clubs at a time when most players had at least twice that many in their bags, he posted a two-over thirty-eight for the back nine and proceeded to shoot sixty-nine in the afternoon round. His thirty-six-hole score of 139 set a new Open record, and he led his nearest competitor, Wilfred Reid, by three strokes.

It seemed for a time that Reid would present a formidable challenge, and he went out in thirty-two at the start of the third round the following morning. But his game suddenly fell apart, and after carding three consecutive sevens, he limped home with a forty-three. Evans, on the other hand, played steadily, and he turned in a seventy-four, three over par on the 6,130-yard track. He was still three shots up after fifty-four holes, and though Reid had fallen back, Evans was now being pressed by Jock Hutchison and Jim Barnes. In fact, it looked like Evans might lose his lead after he took a double bogey seven on the par-five fourth at the beginning of the final round. But he rebounded nicely, carding a birdie on the next hole and completing the front in thirty-seven. He was cruising along the back side when he heard that Hutchison had charged home with a 68. Evans responded to that news

by reaching the par-five, 535-yard twelfth green in two and two-putting for birdie. His afternoon seventy-three gave him a record seventy-two-hole total of 286 and a two-shot victory over Hutchison. His score was the lowest in Open history, a mark that would stand for twenty years.

The 1916 Open was the first major championship hosted by Minikahda, whose original nine-hole course was built by Robert Foulis and Willie Watson in 1899 and later remodeled and transformed into an eighteen-hole track by Robert Taylor and C.T. Jaffray. The U.S. Amateur came to the club in 1927, with Bobby Jones winning that title for the third time. Thirty years later Minikahda hosted the Walker Cup and in 1988 welcomed competitors in the Women's Amateur.

Myopia Hunt Club

1898, 1901, 1905, 1908

It has the strangest name of any Open course in history and is regarded as one of the toughest tracks on which a national championship has ever been played. Yet few people have ever heard of the understated Myopia Hunt Club. That's largely because it is a simple, quiet spot that has long shunned the limelight and hasn't hosted a major golf tournament since 1908. Still, Myopia deserves attention because it is one of only seven courses that have been the site of four or more U.S. Opens.

Myopia was organized in 1875 by Delano Sanborn, a one-time pitcher on the Harvard baseball team and one of four sons of Boston Mayor Frederick Prince. The original club was located in the town of Nahant on a sliver of land that juts into Massachusetts Bay northeast of Boston, and the main athletic activity was lawn tennis. The boys also formed a traveling baseball team, and because several members of the squad were nearsighted and wore glasses—including the four Princes—they called themselves the Myopia Nine. Eventually, that's the moniker they gave their club. They incorporated in 1879 and moved operations to nearby Winchester; four years later the members relocated thirty miles north to South Hamilton.

Early on, lawn tennis and fox hunting were the primary recreations of Myopia club members. But soon they also became interested in golf,

Golf Courses of the U.S. Open

and in 1894 a nine-hole course was designed and built by R.M. Appleton, the master of hounds. The club held its first tournament that June, and the winner was a guest named H.C. Leeds. The former captain of the Harvard football team and a golfing member of The Country Club in nearby Brookline, Leeds was asked to join Myopia in 1896. He was also invited to sit on the club's golf committee, and one of his first tasks was to redo the original nine-hole course. The "Long Nine," as it came to be known, measured 2,928 yards and so pleased Leeds that he petitioned the United States Golf Association to hold the Open there. Two years later, the championship came to Myopia.

The 1898 Open was the first to be contested over seventy-two holes, and golfers played the Long Nine eight times in two days. But not many of them had an easy go of it. J.D. Tucker, for example, recorded the highest score in Open history when he carded a 157 for his first eigh-

A FORMER CAPTAIN OF THE HARVARD FOOTBALL TEAM, H.C. LEEDS, REDESIGNED THE ORIGINAL NINE-HOLE COURSE AT MYOPIA IN TIME FOR THE 1898 OPEN; THE CLUB WOULD GO ON TO HOST THREE MORE CHAMPIONSHIPS.

(TOM DOAK)

teen holes; he managed to knock fifty-seven strokes off his score in his afternoon round but withdrew nonetheless with a thirty-six-hole total of 257. Englishman Fred Herd found the course much more to his liking, however, and he finished at 328 to beat Alex Smith by seven strokes and Willie Anderson by eight. Leeds also played in Myopia's first Open and ended up tied for eighth, nineteen shots back.

Leeds was happy with the way his course held up during the championship, but he was frustrated because the track had only nine holes. So he persuaded the club to purchase some adjoining property, and after visiting the new layout at Shinnecock Hills in Long Island and reading all he could about overseas courses, he put in another nine. One of the problems posed by the terrain of the new course was the stone walls that crisscrossed the fairways. Rather than having the rocks removed altogether, Leeds instructed his workers to stack them in piles around the property and cover them with soil so they would grow grass. When the second nine opened in 1901, members dubbed the large mounds "chocolate drops."

THE SECOND TEE AT MYOPIA LOOKS OVER A SPRAWLING 487-YARD PAR FIVE. A WIN AT THE 1905 OPEN HELD HERE MADE WILLIE ANDERSON THE ONLY GOLFER TO WIN THREE CONSECUTIVE OPENS. (TOM DOAK)

The Open came to Myopia three more times. Willie Anderson won in 1901 with a three-day score of 331, the highest in Open history. Four years later he captured the title again and declared afterward that Myopia "is the best course in the country, if not in the world." In 1908 the diminutive Fred McLeod shot a seventy-seven in the final round to take home the championship trophy.

Rare was the U.S. Open player who broke eighty at Myopia. In fact, four of the five highest winning scores in Open history were recorded at the South Hamilton club. The rough was wire-brush thick, and the greens so slippery that pro Mike Brady took nine putts on one hole alone in 1908. That year another player, Ernie Way, hit a putt that rolled off the green and into a swamp. He never found the ball, making him the only U.S. Open golfer ever to lose his ball on a putt.

A MAP OF THE LONG NINE-HOLE COURSE AS IT LOOKED IN 1898. THE BACK NINE WAS ADDED IN 1901, CREATING ONE OF THE MOST DIFFICULT COURSES IN OPEN HISTORY: FOUR OF THE FIVE HIGHEST WINNING OPEN SCORES EVER WERE RECORDED AT MYOPIA. (USGA)

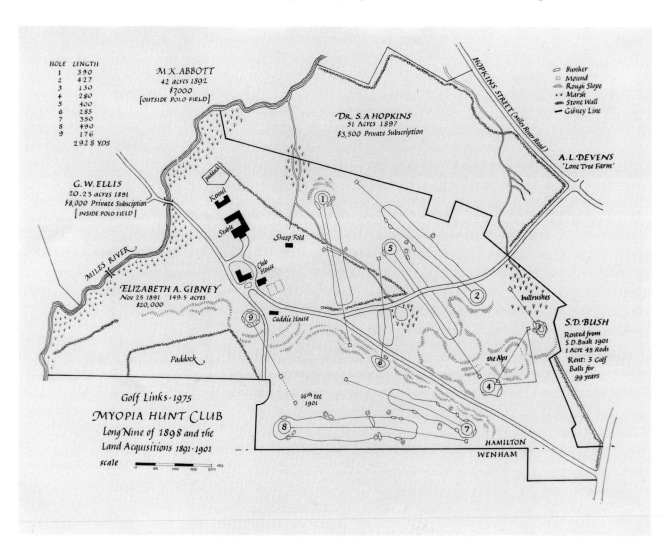

Newport Golf Club

1895

Golf came to Newport, Rhode Island, in 1890 when a group of men led by summer resident Theodore Havemeyer rented forty acres of farmland near Brenton Point and laid out a primitive nine-hole track. Havemeyer had learned about the sport while vacationing in France the previous winter, and it took him and his friends just a few days to build the new course, which was one of the first in America. Fences and stone walls crossed the land at several points, and although they often interferred with play, there was nothing the golfers could do about them because the lease did not allow for any alterations of the property.

WHITNEY WARREN DESIGNED THE SUMPTUOUS NEWPORT CLUBHOUSE, WHICH OPENED IN 1895, A FEW MONTHS BEFORE THE INAUGURAL U.S. OPEN. (LARRY LAMBRECHT)

The game quickly became a favorite among the area's elite, and in the winter of 1893, they founded the Newport Golf Club. Havemeyer was named president, and the board of governors included Frederick W. Vanderbilt, Lorillard Spencer, and E.R. Wharton. Fifty-seven charter members were elected at a meeting that spring, and the nearby Bateman Hotel was leased for use as a clubhouse.

Members of the new club played the Brenton Point layout that first year, but in 1894 they purchased another farm and had their head professional, William F. Davis, build a new nine-hole course as well as a six-hole track for beginners. They also constructed an elegant clubhouse of their own. Designed by Whitney Warren in the shape of a propeller, with two main wings running north and south and a piazza extending to the east, it was an impressive building that received numerous accolades, including one from *The New York Times* saying it "stood supreme for magnificence among golf clubs, not only in America but in the world."

The clubhouse opened in the spring of 1895, and that year Newport, which had joined four other clubs the previous winter in

THE COURSE AT NEWPORT HAS CHANGED A LOT OVER THE YEARS, BUT GOLFERS TODAY MUST STILL BATTLE THE SAME ATLANTIC WINDS FACED BY HORACE RAWLINS, WINNER OF THE FIRST U.S. OPEN. (LARRY LAMBRECHT)

forming what is now the United States Golf Association, hosted America's first official amateur and open championships. The tournaments were originally scheduled to take place in September but were postponed a month because of a scheduling conflict with a more established Newport spectacle, the America's Cup yacht races. Charles Blair Macdonald won the Amateur, twelve and eleven, and the following day the Newport Golf Club assistant, a twenty-one-year-old Englishman named Horace Rawlins, captured the first Open title. He made four trips around the nine-hole course in 173, beating Willie Dunn by two strokes. It was a bittersweet defeat for Dunn. The previous year he had won a national open tournament at the St. Andrew's Golf Club in Yonkers,

NEWPORT'S TREACHEROUS BUNKERS HAVEN'T PLAGUED OPEN GOLFERS SINCE 1895. BUT FOR ITS HUNDREDTH ANNIVERSARY, THE COURSE HOSTED THE 1995 U.S. AMATEUR. (LARRY LAMBRECHT)

New York, and received one hundred dollars and a gold medal. The victory, Dunn thought, made him the country's first Open titlist, but many well-regarded golfers, including Macdonald, felt that no single club could arbitrarily decide a true national championship. That conflict led to the formation of the USGA, which officially sanctioned the 1895 amateur and open competitions and resolved much of the controversy. But it took something dear away from Dunn, who never won an official Open but proudly wore his medal from St. Andrew's until the day he died in 1925.

The Newport course has undergone several changes over the years. William Davis revamped some of his original "long" course prior to the 1895 Open, turning it into a 2,755-yard, par thirty-five layout, with six par fours, one par five and two par threes. An additional nine holes were added in 1897, and then Donald Ross made significant modifications in the early part of the twentieth century. Further additions were made in the 1920s when the club purchased a piece of adjoining land and asked A.W. Tillinghast to reroute some of the old course and design seven new holes. The club has never hosted another Open, but it was the site of one of the first Senior PGA events as well as the 1995 U.S. Amateur, which was won by Tiger Woods.

North Shore Country Club

1933

When North Shore Country Club opened its doors in 1900, it was known as the Ouilmette Country Club, which boasted a five-hole course that the members had built themselves on a vacant lot in a village north of Chicago. In 1908 a clubhouse fire forced a move to a new site in Kenilworth, which the members leased for the next fifteen years. They incorporated there and adopted their current moniker. The club stayed at Kenilworth until 1923, when it bought 170 acres of land in nearby Glenview and settled in its present location.

One of the first orders of business at the new address was hiring a pair of architects, Charles Hugh Alison and Harry Shapland Colt, to

build a new golf course. It didn't take long for them to complete the task, and on May 31, 1924, the North Shore Country Club officially opened on its new site. The highly regarded course hosted the Western Open four years later. Five years after that, the United States Golf Association brought its signature event to the club. Tommy Armour was the first-round leader, shooting sixty-eight on the par seventy-two, 6,927-yard layout and ending up five strokes ahead of his nearest competitors. While Armour struggled to a seventy-five the following day, an amateur from Omaha, Nebraska, named Johnny Goodman scorched the North Shore layout and posted a sixty-six, which tied Gene Sarazen's eighteen-hole record and put him in the lead by two shots.

Goodman hit only twenty-five putts the entire second round, and his stroke was almost as smooth the next day as he posted a seventy for

THE NORTH SHORE COUNTRY CLUB MOVED AROUND A BIT IN ITS EARLY YEARS BEFORE SETTLING ON ITS CURRENT SITE IN 1924. JOHNNY GOODMAN'S OPEN VICTORY THERE IN 1933 MARKED THE LAST TIME AN AMATEUR WON A U.S. OPEN. (USGA)

THE COURSE DESIGN AT NORTH SHORE REMAINS CLOSE TO THAT OF THE 1933 OPEN. THE GLENVIEW, ILLINOIS, CLUB ALSO HOSTED THE AMATEUR IN 1939 AND 1983. (USGA)

a six-shot lead of 211 after fifty-four holes. Goodman opened the final round par-eagle-birdie and seemed ready for a romp. But he soon tensed up and, after carding thirty-nine on the front, was only two strokes ahead of Ralph Guldahl at the start of the back nine. Somehow, Goodman got it back, and he reeled off four quick pars. A bogey at fourteen hurt, but he recovered with a bird on fifteen and went in par-bogey-par for a seventy-six. Guldahl was playing behind him and, after making five straight pars on the back, walked up the eighteenth fairway with a chance to win or tie the tournament. A birdie would give him the Open trophy, and a par would give him the opportunity to fight it out in a play-off the next day. Guldahl hit his approach on eighteen into a greenside bunker. He blasted out to within four feet but missed his putt and his chance at the title. That made Goodman a winner, the fifth and last amateur to reign as U.S. Open champion.

Goodman was only twenty-three years old at the time of his victory. One of ten children, he came from a poor family, and after his mother died, he had been forced to drop out of school to support his siblings. One of the jobs he took was caddying at the Omaha Field Club, and Goodman got good enough at the game that he rode a cattle car out west in 1929 to play in the U.S. Amateur at Pebble Beach. One of his opponents was Bobby Jones, and Goodman beat the Georgia gentleman one up. He didn't turn pro until after he had won the 1937 U.S. Amateur. But he never enjoyed much success on the golf course after that.

North Shore hosted the U.S. Amateur two years after Goodman captured that title and hosted it again in 1983. The basic course design remains much as it was for the '33 Open, with the exception of some longer holes, a few enlarged greens, and three new lakes.

Northwood Club

1952

Located in Dallas, the Northwood Club opened in 1948 and hosted the U.S. Open four years later. The par seventy, 6,782-yard course was designed by William Diddel and at the time was considered one of the toughest in the land. The pros certainly had their share of troubles with it during the 1952 championship; few of them broke par on any of the rounds.

Ben Hogan didn't have any problems early on. After winning at Merion and Oakland Hills the previous two years, the Hawk was looking for his third Open title in a row and came out smoking, carding back-to-back sixty-nines and tying a thirty-six-hole scoring record. Hogan held a two-stroke lead over George Fazio at the beginning of play Saturday morning. But he wilted in the sweltering heat, posting a seventy-four for his first round that day and dropping into second. The man who took his place at the head of the pack was Julius Boros, who had shot 68 after opening the tournament with a pair of seventy-ones.

Boros seemed an unlikely leader. A native of Fairfield, Connecticut, who had worked for many years as an accountant, he had left his business to turn pro in 1950 when he was twenty-nine years old. He had a graceful swing, an easy temperament, and didn't linger over his shots. He finished first in a handful of regional tournaments as an amateur but had yet to win anything on the PGA Tour.

That, however, was about to change. Paired with Lew Worsham, Boros shot even par for the front nine Saturday afternoon and had seven one putts on the back for another seventy-one. He hit only eleven putts on the entire back nine that afternoon and a remarkable twenty-nine for the whole eighteen. His four-round total of 281 gave him the Open

JULIUS BOROS PULLED AWAY FROM THE PACK IN THE THIRD ROUND TO WIN THE 1952 OPEN AT NORTHWOOD BY FOUR STROKES. (NORTHWOOD CLUB)

crown by four shots. Ed "Porky" Oliver posted a final-round seventy-two for a score of 285 and second place, while Hogan stumbled in with another seventy-four to finish five back at 286. Johnny Bulla ended up fourth, and Fazio took fifth, nine shots out.

The 1952 Open was Boros's first Tour victory, and he would win another national championship at The Country Club in Brookline in 1963. He also won the 1968 PGA when he was forty-eight years old. At fifty-five he almost became the oldest winner on the regular Tour when he lost a play-off with Gene Littler at the 1975 Westchester Classic. A stalwart on the Seniors Tour for many years, Boros died in the spring of 1994, shortly after his seventy-fourth birthday.

AT THE TIME OF THE 1952 OPEN, NORTHWOOD'S WILLIAM DIDDEL-DESIGNED COURSE, WITH ITS DEEP ROUGH, BENT GRASS FAIRWAYS, AND LONG HOLES, WAS CONSIDERED AMONG THE MOST DIFFICULT IN THE COUNTRY. (NORTHWOOD CLUB)

Oak Hill Country Club

1956, 1968, 1989

It all began in 1901 when twenty-five golfers from the Rochester, New York, area started a country club known as Oak Hill. They leased eighty-five acres of farmland bordering the Genesee River and laid out a simple nine-hole golf course. An old farmhouse was used as a clubhouse, and a nearby barn served as the locker room. Each member paid an initiation fee of twenty-five dollars, and dues were set at twenty dollars a year. The club prospered, and in 1905 the members bought the land they had been renting. Five years later another nine holes were added, and in 1911 a new clubhouse opened.

Things at Oak Hill were going so well that it came as a shock to members when the University of Rochester decided to expand its campus and wondered if the club would be willing to give up its property. Lengthy talks followed, and an agreement was eventually reached: in exchange for the land, the university would finance the design and construction of two new golf courses and a clubhouse on 355 acres of farmland in suburban Pittsford.

At first it looked as if the members of Oak Hill got the short end of the stick, because the ragged land they had acquired was almost completely devoid of trees. The club called in architect Donald Ross for a consultation, and at a meeting in 1922, he told members that the site could be made into "one of the finest golf courses in the United States." He described the area as one of "remarkable beauty," referring in particular to the rolling land and the creek that meandered through the fields and woods. The club quickly enlisted Ross's services, and he began construction in 1924. Two years later, the East and West Courses were open for play.

Ross built the golf courses that gave Oak Hill its character, but it was a physician named John Williams who planted the trees that gave the club its identity. A longtime member and self-taught botanist, Williams made it his personal project to cover the club grounds with trees. He planted seeds in his backyard and raised them to saplings, which he then transferred to the property. His work on Oak Hill soon became so well known that people from all over the world began send-

ing him seeds and acorns. One came from a tree planted by George Washington, for example, and another from the Shakespeare Oak in Stratford-on-Avon, England. Over the years, Williams almost single-handedly transformed the barren farmland into an arboretum, and today the Oak Hill property boasts some eighty thousand trees, just under half of them on the championship East Course.

Maybe it was all those trees that had kept the club hidden from view, but regardless, Oak Hill was a fairly obscure spot in northern New York when United States Golf Association executive director Joe Dey paid a visit in 1948. "Where have you been for twenty years?" he asked

THE FINISHING HOLE AT OAK HILL, A PAR-FOUR DOGLEG RIGHT, IS AS HEAVILY BUNKERED AND TREED AS ANY HOLE ON THE COURSE—IT ALSO ENDS AT THE NARROWEST GREEN. (ROBERT WALKER)

LEE TREVINO CAPTURED HIS FIRST TOUR
VICTORY AT THE 1968 OPEN AT OAK
HILL, BEATING JACK NICKLAUS OUT
SOUNDLY BY FOUR STROKES.

the club officers when they met. "There's nothing like this in the whole
country." A year later Oak Hill hosted the U.S. Amateur, and in 1956 it
was the site of the U.S. Open.

As it prepared for its Open debut, the club brought in architect
Robert Trent Jones to make several changes, mostly with an eye toward
toughening the track. A Rochester native who knew Oak Hill well, Jones

added more than two dozen bunkers, altered the design of at least that many others, lengthened the layout some 350 yards, and dropped par from seventy-two to seventy. But the basic nature of Ross's work remained, and the course held up well. No one broke par in the first round that year, and Cary Middlecoff's winning score was a one-over 281.

The pros were a little rougher on Oak Hill in 1968. Bert Yancey fired sixty-seven and sixty-eight the first two rounds and led Lee Trevino by two strokes after thirty-six holes. Playing in only his third Open, Trevino shot a pair of sixty-nines the final two days and beat Jack Nicklaus by four shots for his first Tour win. His seventy-two-hole score of 275 tied an Open record that had been set by the Golden Bear, and he became the first man in a national championship to shoot all four rounds in the sixties.

That did not please the USGA, and the organization turned down Oak Hill's request for a third Open several years later. Clearly, the course needed to be strengthened again, so the club asked designers George and Tom Fazio for their help. Beginning in 1976, the Fazios redesigned holes six and fifteen and made major alterations on five and eighteen. Reactions to the changes were mixed: some thought the feel of the original Ross layout had been destroyed, while others believed that the Fazios had made it better. The PGA of America liked what it saw and

voted to hold its championship at the club in 1980. It wasn't long before the USGA weighed in as well, announcing that it was bringing the Open back to Oak Hill in 1989.

The club was thrilled with the news, but everything it had done to make the course more Open-ready seemed to be for naught as heavy rains softened the greens and helped produce thirty-eight under-par rounds the first two days. The leader after thirty-six holes was Curtis Strange, who had posted a spectacular sixty-four on Friday. He fell back to third, three strokes behind Tom Kite, after shooting seventy-three the next day. But as Kite tumbled on Sunday, Strange carded a seventy to earn his second U.S. Open title in a row. The last person to do that was Ben Hogan in 1950 and 1951.

Oak Hill is not yet scheduled to hold another Open, but after a good tournament in 1989 and a successful Ryder Cup six years later, it has certainly earned another shot. Until then, the members will keep themselves busy planning for another major championship, the U.S. Amateur, which will be held there in 1998.

Oakland Hills Country Club

1924, 1937, 1951, 1961, 1985, 1996

When architect Donald Ross surveyed a stretch of land some eighteen miles northwest of Detroit in 1916, he said simply, "The Lord intended this for a golf links." Then he built two courses on the property, one of which the Lord must have intended for the U.S. Open. It was the South Course at the Oakland Hills Country Club in Birmingham, Michigan, and it would go on to host six national championships by the end of the century. Only Baltusrol and Oakmont would host more.

Oakland Hills was created by a Ford sales executive, Norval Hawkins, and his accountant friend, Joseph Mack. They had invested in a real estate venture outside the Detroit suburb and thought for a

AFTER ROBERT TRENT JONES REMODELED OAKLAND HILLS' DONALD ROSS DESIGN FOR THE 1951 U.S. OPEN, THE PLENTIFUL BUNKERS, SMALL GREENS, AND WATER HAZARDS—LIKE THOSE SEEN HERE ON SIXTEEN—EARNED THE COURSE THE NICKNAME "THE MONSTER."
(ROBERT WALKER)

THE PAR-FOUR TENTH AT OAKLAND HILLS MEASURES 454 YARDS. AT THE OPEN THERE IN 1985, ANDY NORTH EDGED OUT TAIWANESE COMPETITOR T.C. CHEN BY ONE STROKE AFTER CHEN TOOK A QUADRUPLE-BOGEY EIGHT ON THE FIFTH. (ROBERT WALKER)

while about building houses there. But as the game of golf became more and more popular, they decided instead to create a country club where carmakers working in the Motor City could socialize in style. They hired Donald Ross to design and build the courses, and the club opened in 1917. The pro shop was housed in an old chicken coop, and the first head professional was the great Walter Hagen, who had won the U.S. Open three years before. The Haig hung around for a couple of years, spending far more time perfecting his own swing than working with the club members. After winning a second Open in 1919, he quit to go back on tour full-time. His replacement was a fellow named Mike Brady, another touring pro whom Hagen had just beaten in a play-off for his most recent Open title.

Oakland Hills didn't have to wait long for an Open of its own, with the first one arriving in 1924. Having captured the championship at Inwood the year before, Bobby Jones was considered the favorite, and he played like one for fifty-four holes, finishing the third round tied for the lead with a relative unknown, Cyril Walker. An agonizingly slow golfer who weighed less than 120 pounds, Walker surprised everyone by shooting seventy-five for the last eighteen while Jones carded a seventy-eight, and the slight Englishman so adept at scrambling took home the championship trophy that many had conceded to the Georgia amateur at the start of play.

The tournament came back to Oakland Hills in 1937, and that was the year Sam Snead made his Open debut. And what an entrance. Snead shot sixty-nine for the first-round lead, and he stayed near the top of the board the rest of the way. His seventy-two-hole score was 283, and as he sat in the locker room that afternoon, Tommy Armour approached him and said, "Laddie, you've just won yourself the Open." But he hadn't. Ralph Guldahl had teed off about an hour behind Snead and, after shooting a three-under-par thirty-three on the front, carded a par thirty-six on the back for a sixty-nine and a two-stroke win over the rookie. Sadly, that would not be the only time Snead came short in an Open.

Ben Hogan never had much trouble with national championships. He collected four Open titles over the years, including one at Oakland Hills in 1951. The South Course had been renovated by Robert Trent Jones prior to that event, and he built a slew of new bunkers and shrunk some of the greens. He also shortened the course 110 yards and reduced par from seventy-two to seventy, while the United States Golf Association tightened the fairways. Many observers felt that the finished product was the most intimidating Open course in history, and Willard Mullin of the *New York World Telegram* dubbed it "The Monster." But

BEN HOGAN SHOT A 67 IN THE LAST ROUND OF THE 1951 OPEN TO CAPTURE HIS SECOND TITLE IN A ROW. ALTHOUGH HOGAN WENT ON TO WIN TWO MORE OPENS, HE LATER SAID THAT HIS FINAL EIGHTEEN AT OAKLAND HILLS WAS THE FINEST ROUND OF HIS CAREER. (USGA)

the Hawk never saw anything montsrous about the layout. In fact, he capped a fine tournament by shooting sixty-seven for the final eighteen. It was Hogan's second Open title in a row, and he later said that his Saturday afternoon round was the greatest he had ever played.

Gene Littler won Oakland Hills's fourth Open in 1961, holding off Doug Sanders and Bob Goalby. And twenty-four years later the championship came back to Birmingham. The 1985 tournament seemed to revolve around the successes and failures of a diminutive Taiwanese gentleman named T.C. Chen. Thanks to a strong putting stroke and a double eagle on the second hole, Chen held the lead for the first three days and was four strokes up on Andy North for the tournament after playing four holes on Sunday. But disaster awaited him at the fifth hole. He double-hit his ball on a wedge shot and ended up taking a quadruple-bogey eight, falling suddenly into a tie with North. To his credit, Chen battled back and even managed to grab the lead again. But in the end it was North who came out on top, with Chen tied for second, one shot back.

Tom Watson threatened in his first
major in several years at the 1996
Open at Oakland Hills, finishing a
respectable fourth. (Pat Seelig)

After hosting the 1996 Open, which was won by Steve Jones,
Oakland Hills began its wait for the USGA to give it its seventh championship sometime early in the twenty-first century. Although it has
undergone some minor alterations since Robert Trent Jones worked on
it before the '51 Open, the South Course remains pretty much as it was
when Hogan won. A fair and tough track, to be sure. But certainly not
a monster.

Oakmont Country Club

1927, 1935, 1953, 1962, 1973, 1983, 1994

THE FAMOUS CHURCH PEW BUNKER BETWEEN THE THIRD AND FOURTH HOLES AT OAKMONT HAS PLAGUED GOLFERS IN SEVEN U.S. OPENS SINCE THE CLUB HOSTED ITS FIRST IN 1927. (USGA)

Henry Fownes was a Pittsburgh steel tycoon who knew nothing about golf until his friend Andrew Carnegie introduced him to the sport in 1899. He took it up with a passion and became good enough to compete in four U.S. Amateurs. He liked the game so much that he decided to build his own golf club, and in 1904 he founded the Oakmont Country

Club. It was a modest spot at the time, but by the end of the twentieth century it had hosted more men's championship tournaments—seven U.S. Opens, four U.S. Amateurs, and three PGAs—than any other course in America.

Although his knowledge of architecture was limited, Fownes designed Oakmont himself. His goal was to create the hardest course possible, and he wanted to model it after a British moorland track. He laid it out on a barren plateau high above the Allegheny River and generously sprinkled it with sand bunkers, 220 in all. As much as he wanted to, Fownes could not put in traditional pot bunkers because the clay-rich soil of western Pennsylvania drained poorly. So he kept the ones at Oakmont shallow but devised an almost sinister way of toughening them by making a special rake with triangular teeth that was weighted with a hundred-pound slab of steel. He used that tool to carve furrows in the sand that were three inches deep and ran perpendicular to the play of the hole. That made almost every bunker shot seem like a buried lie, and in most cases, all a player could do was blast out and sacrifice a stroke.

JACK NICKLAUS WATCHES INTENTLY AS ARNOLD PALMER PUTTS DURING THE 1962 OPEN. WHEN THE TWENTY-TWO-YEAR-OLD NICKLAUS SURPRISED OBSERVERS BY MATCHING THE HIGHLY FAVORED PALMER'S 283, TEN THOUSAND PEOPLE TURNED OUT FOR THE PLAY-OFF—NICKLAUS CLAIMED HIS FIRST PROFESSIONAL VICTORY BY THREE STROKES. (USGA)

HENRY CLAY FOWNES'S ORIGINAL 1903 DESIGN AT OAKMONT INCORPORATED MORE THAN 350 BUNKERS. HE BELIEVED THAT "A SHOT POORLY PLAYED SHOULD BE A SHOT IRREVOCABLY LOST." THE NUMBER OF BUNKERS HAS BEEN GRADUALLY REDUCED SINCE THAT TIME—THERE WERE ONLY 180 AT THE 1994 OPEN. (USGA)

The greens at Oakmont were just as tough because they were cut short and rolled. They were so fast that as Kerr Petrie, a writer for the *New York Herald Tribune*, watched a team of Fownes's men pushing a fifteen hundred-pound roller across a green one day, he said to a worker, "Why don't you just dig them up and pour in concrete?"

Fownes watched over his new course like a father and often consulted his son, Bill, when it came time to make improvements. Fownes the younger was a talented golfer in his own right, and he qualified for twenty-five U.S. Amateurs, winning in 1910. In time, he took over his

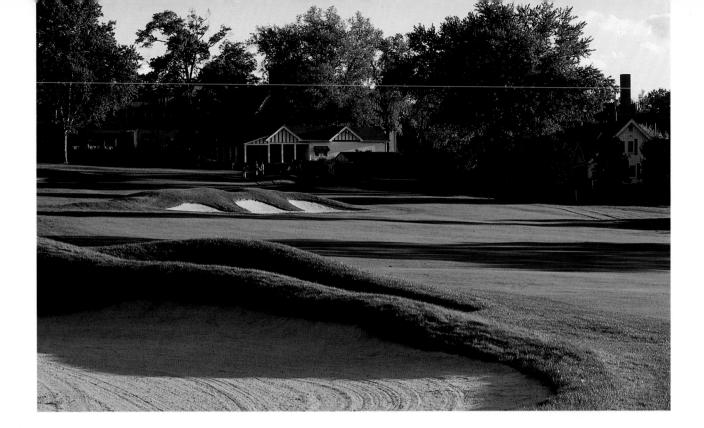

father's role as the Oakmont watchdog. He would periodically wander the course, and if he saw someone boom a drive over a bunker, for example, he would instruct the greenskeeper to put in another one. Fownes did that so many times that Oakmont was soon pocked with some 350 bunkers, his theory being that "a shot poorly played should be a shot irrevocably lost."

Oakmont hosted its first major tournament in 1919 when the U.S. Amateur came to town, and Bill Fownes made it all the way to the semi-finals before losing to seventeen-year-old Bobby Jones. The club hosted the PGA Championship in 1922, a second Amateur in 1925, and two years later the United States Golf Association brought the U.S. Open to Oakmont for the first time.

Oakmont was a par seventy-two, 6,929-yard course when the national championship was held there in 1927, and the winning score of 301 was the highest in modern history. Tommy Armour and "Lighthorse" Harry Cooper shared the lead after seventy-two holes, but Armour prevailed in a play-off, seventy-six to seventy-nine.

Eight years later the Open returned, and the scores were not much better. A number of players made a run at the title, but it was little-known Sam Parks Jr., who was left standing at the end. An Ohio native who had taken lessons as a boy from Gene Sarazen, Parks had been serving as the head professional at the nearby South Hills Country Club and knew a little bit about the Oakmont course. In fact, he got up early every day for a month before the Open so he could play nine holes at

THE LENGTH, GRADE, AND LIBERAL BUNKERING MAKE DOUBLE BOGEYS ON THE 456-YARD, UPHILL, PAR-FOUR EIGHTEENTH ALL TOO COMMON.
(ROBERT WALKER)

Oakmont before work. Parks never won another tournament and quit teaching golf in 1942 to take a job with U.S. Steel.

There was nothing obscure about the winner of Oakmont's next Open in 1953. His name was Ben Hogan, and he battled Sam Snead for four rounds to win his fourth and final Open title. The Hawk's seventy-two-hole score of 283 was much lower than the scores of the previous two Opens at Oakmont, but it also came after the club had stopped using Fownes's furrowed rakes in the bunkers. For Snead, 1953 was the fourth time he had been runner-up in the national championship. The tournament also marked the Open debut of a young amateur from nearby Latrobe named Arnold Palmer. He missed the cut after shooting eighty-four and seventy-eight and went quietly away.

But Palmer was back when the Open returned in 1962, and he fought an epic battle with twenty-two-year-old Jack Nicklaus. They were paired the first two rounds, and Arnold led by three shots after thirty-six holes. But he fell back during the final thirty-six, and they ended up tied. Nicklaus quickly went up by four shots in the play-off and never looked back, posting a seventy-one to Arnold's seventy-four for his first Open win.

Mention Oakmont 1973, and only one name comes to mind: Johnny Miller. He arrived at the club Sunday morning six off the lead and tied for thirteenth, having shot seventy-six the day before. But he birdied the first four holes and went on to play the greatest final round in major championship history. Miller went out in thirty-two and came back in thirty-one for a sixty-three and a one-stroke win over John Schlee. No golfer was supposed to manhandle Oakmont like that, and legend has it that Lew Worsham, the club pro and 1947 Open champion, was heard muttering, "Lie still, Mr. Fownes, lie still," as he walked across the grounds that night. Not surprisingly, the club asked Arnold Palmer and his design partner, Ed Seay, to come in shortly afterward and put some fight back into the grand old course.

Oakmont has hosted two other Opens, but neither had the pure drama and excitement of Miller's win in 1973. Larry Nelson came out on top in 1983, carding a sixty-seven Sunday afternoon to hold off Tom Watson. And in 1994, South African Ernie Els defeated Loren Roberts and Colin Montgomerie in a play-off.

Major championships have come and gone, but not much has changed at Oakmont since its founding. The club is nearly a century old and, in 1987, became the first course in America to be declared a national historic landmark. It may have some age to it, but Oakmont is still as tough a test of golf as can be found in this country, which is good because Henry Fownes wouldn't have wanted it any other way.

Olympia Fields Country Club

1928

Like so many country clubs before it, Olympia Fields was born from the vision of a man who loved golf. His name was Charles Beach, and one autumn afternoon in 1913 he took a hike through a beautiful section of

TEN YEARS AFTER OPENING IN 1915, OLYMPIA FIELDS COUNTRY CLUB BOASTED FOUR GOLF COURSES. THE 1928 OPEN WAS PLAYED ON THE NORTH COURSE, PICTURED HERE. BUTTERFIELD CREEK WINDS THROUGHOUT THE COURSE, FACTORING HEAVILY INTO GOLFERS' APPROACH STRATEGIES. (ACME)

rolling meadows and woods about thirty miles south of Chicago. Here, he thought, was a perfect site for not only one but several golf courses. And he began to think of how one day, people could enjoy a variety of sports at a vast club in this area.

Beach walked around that land for most of the afternoon and then came back the following two days. On his third visit he brought a friend, James Gardner, and the two of them spent several hours climbing hills, wandering around cornfields, wading through creeks, and scrambling under barbed wire fences. Gardner was as taken with the property as Beach was, and as night began to fall, they agreed to try to build a country club there. By 1915 a club charter had been written and signed, and a president, the famed college football player and coach Amos Alonzo Stagg, appointed. A year later members had begun playing golf on what was to be the first of four courses built on the seven hundred-odd acres that they owned.

THE LURKING CREEK, NUMEROUS BUNKERS, AND UPHILL APPROACH SHOT MAKE THIS AN IMPOSING HOLE AT OLYMPIA FIELDS. (PAT SEELIG)

OLYMPIA FIELDS' STATELY CLUBHOUSE
WAS BUILT IN THE MID 1920S. IN ITS
HEYDAY THE STRUCTURE OVERLOOKED
750 ACRES WITH SEVENTY-TWO HOLES
OF GOLF, FIFTY SUMMER HOMES, A
HOSPITAL, SCHOOL, AND FIRE STATION.

(PAT SEELIG)

They wasted little time in creating a spectacular facility, and by 1922 Olympia Fields featured four eighteen-hole courses. The first, known as No. 1, was designed by Scotsman Tom Bendelow. Willie Watson laid out the second one, which opened in the spring of 1918, and then he and Bendelow collaborated on No. 3. It opened in June 1920 but later required considerable revision, most of which was handled by club pro Jack Daray. And finally the championship course, No. 4, was constructed by Willie Park, Jr., who claimed he had never worked on better terrrain. Each of No. 4's nines begin in fairly open country, but the tree-lined fairways quickly narrow, so any errant shot means trouble. Perhaps the most famous hole on the course, which has been the site of five Western Opens as well as two PGA Championships and one U.S. Open, is the 429-yard par-four fourteenth. From a pulpit tee, a player must carry Butterfield Creek, which flows into the woods and then reappears farther down the fairway. A second shot must clear that creek again and then hold a slick green, which is well-guarded by traps.

Olympia Fields thrived during the 1920s, and perhaps its finest golfing moment came in 1928 when it hosted the Open. Bobby Jones had won two of the previous four Opens and was considered one of the favorites. He lived up to expectations the first two rounds, shooting seventy-three and seventy-one and jumping out to a thirty-six-hole lead. After carding a seventy-three the morning of the second day, Jones still stood in first place. But he struggled to a seventy-seven in the afternoon and ended up tied with Johnny Farrell.

The two men met in a thirty-six-hole play-off the following day. Farrell led by three strokes—seventy to seventy-three—after the morning round, but was down a stroke after twelve holes in the afternoon. A birdie at thirteen brought him back to even, and when Jones missed a three-foot putt at sixteen, Farrell retook the lead. They both birdied the final two holes, and Farrell had his only Open title.

Olympia Fields changed a great deal after that event, mostly as a result of financial pressure brought on by the Depression. Most of the land that made up courses No. 2 and No. 3 were sold to real estate developers in the 1930s, and the club today boasts only thirty-six holes: the North course, which is the old No. 4, and the South, which was once No. 1.

The Olympic Club

1955, 1966, 1987, 1998

There is something spooky about the Lake Course at the Olympic Club in San Francisco, and if you don't believe that, ask Ben Hogan about how his dreams for a record fifth U.S. Open title were crushed there by a journeyman named Jack Fleck. Or Arnold Palmer, who lost seven shots in nine holes and the championship one Sunday afternoon. Or Tom Watson, the Stanford grad who spent his college days playing Olympic but didn't know the track well enough to avoid bogeying three of the last five holes in 1987. Or sports columnist Jim Murray, who once

Golf Courses of the U.S. Open

described the Lake Course as "a 6,700-yard haunted house. If it were human, it'd be Bela Lugosi. I think it turns into a bat at midnight. It's public enemy number one. Al Capone. John Wilkes Booth."

Olympic has been a nightmare for some of the game's best golfers, and that's too bad because it really is a congenial spot that gives most visitors great pleasure. Olympic traces its beginnings to 1860 when two brothers, Arthur and Charles Nahl, started an athletic club in the basement of their San Francisco home. The organization grew over the years, but golf didn't become part of the program until the early part of the twentieth century when members bought several hundred acres of land on the western edge of town. For a while, the club used a Wilfred Reid course that had already been built on the site. But in 1924 they created two tracks of their own, one of which was the Lake Course, where all

IN THE 1966 OPEN AT OLYMPIC, ARNOLD PALMER SQUANDERED A SEVEN-SHOT LEAD OVER BILLY CASPER IN THE FINAL NINE HOLES. CASPER TRIUMPHED BY FOUR STROKES IN THE PLAY-OFF. (USGA)

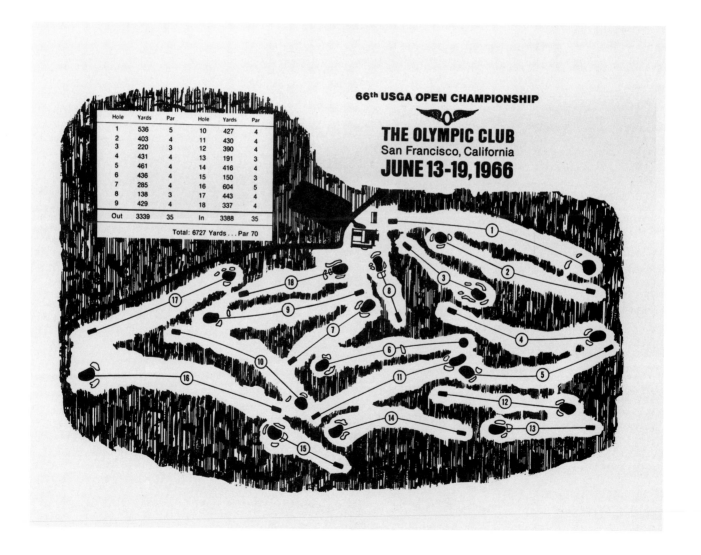

66th USGA OPEN CHAMPIONSHIP

THE OLYMPIC CLUB
San Francisco, California
JUNE 13-19, 1966

Hole	Yards	Par	Hole	Yards	Par
1	536	5	10	427	4
2	403	4	11	430	4
3	220	3	12	390	4
4	431	4	13	191	3
5	461	4	14	416	4
6	436	4	15	150	3
7	285	4	16	604	5
8	138	3	17	443	4
9	429	4	18	337	4
Out	3339	35	In	3388	35

Total: 6727 Yards . . . Par 70

the Opens have been played. Sam Whiting and Willie Watson handled the design work, and they incorporated several holes from the original course into their new layouts, which were built on the inland side of a stretch of sandhills half a mile from the Pacific Ocean.

Initially, Olympic was a links-style course with few trees. But thousands were planted over the years, and by the time the U.S. Open came to town in 1955, the fairways were lined with thick bunches of pine, eucalyptus, redwood, cedar, and cypress. Tommy Bolt took the first-round lead, and he was tied with Harvie Ward at 144 after thirty-six holes. But Ben Hogan overtook them both in Saturday morning's round with a two-over-par seventy-two. After the Hawk carded a seventy for the afternoon, he went into the locker room for a scotch. NBC signed off on its telecast shortly afterward, saying that Hogan had won his fifth Open. Hogan himself was so confident of his position that he gave his

OLYMPIC'S LUXURIOUS LAKE COURSE IS A FAVORITE AMONG FORMER OPEN CHAMPIONS. SAN FRANCISCO'S MOIST CLIMATE PRODUCES LUSH FAIRWAYS THAT SOFTEN BOUNCES AND HINDER ROLLS. (USGA)

BY THE TIME ROBERT TRENT JONES REMODELED OLYMPIC IN THE EARLY 1950S, THE COURSE'S 30,000 TREES HAD GROWN THICK, HEMMING IN THE FAIRWAYS. JONES INCORPORATED THIS CORRIDOR EFFECT INTO HIS DESIGN, MAKING STRAIGHT, ACCURATE SHOTS ESSENTIAL. (TOM DOAK)

ball to United States Golf Association director Joe Dey and said, "This is for Golf House." But Jack Fleck hadn't conceded a thing. He birdied fifteen, parred sixteen and seventeen, and after hitting his approach shot to within six feet on eighteen, putted out for a sixty-seven. That tied him with Hogan after seventy-two holes. In the play-off the next day Fleck wore the Texan out, posting a sixty-nine for a stunning three-stroke win.

The shock from that upset had barely worn off the golfing world when Arnold Palmer arrived at Olympic in 1966 to try for his second Open title. The King was tied for the lead after 36 holes and went into the final round with a three-stroke advantage over Billy Casper. He shot lights out on the front, and his 32 put him up by seven with nine to go. But he started thinking about breaking Hogan's Open record of 276 instead of concentrating on the tournament at hand, and the wheels came flying off. Palmer played the back four over par while Casper shot three under, and the two ended the afternoon tied. Casper prevailed in the play-off, carding a sixty-nine, while Palmer fell apart again on the back nine to finish with a seventy-three.

Tom Watson didn't have anything quite so awful happen to him in 1987. But he did bogey three of the last five holes to lose by a stroke to Scott Simpson. Watson had needed a birdie on eighteen to force a play-off, and his approach shot to the green at the 343-yard par four looked for a moment as if it would cover the pin. But the ball came up short and then spun backward to the front collar some thirty-five feet away. Watson stroked a smooth putt to the hole, but it just missed.

It seems strange sometimes that Olympic would treat the pros so harshly. Just 6,700 yards, it is the shortest among all active Open courses. It has no water hazards, only one fairway bunker, and players can bump-and-run to all but three greens. But the moist San Francisco air keeps the grass wet, which takes distance off of drives and makes the rough even rougher. The course also has a plethora of trees, hills, and doglegs as well as a dozen par fours averaging over four hundred yards, all of which make it deceptively difficult and a favorite among the folks at the USGA. In fact, they are bringing the Open back to Olympic in 1998. It will be interesting to see who the next victim is.

THE 480-YARD, PAR-FOUR SEVENTEENTH IS ONE OF THE MOST INTIMIDATING HOLES AT OLYMPIC. (TOM DOAK)

Onwentsia Club

1906

Lake Forest was a conservative Presbyterian town when Charles Blair Macdonald visited one weekend in 1892. He had come to introduce some of the locals to a new game called golf which he picked up while studying at the University of St. Andrews in Scotland. Using empty tomato cans as cups, he laid out a seven-hole course on the lawn of Senator Charles Farwell's lakefront home and began demonstrating how the sport was played. It caught on quickly, and the estate soon became a popular recreational retreat for the area's fledgling golfers.

It wasn't long, however, before those golfers outgrew that site some thirty miles north of Chicago, and in 1894 they laid out a new nine-hole course on a nearby farm. There weren't any bunkers, but the course featured several other hazards, including a treacherous water hole and a large number of sheep, as well as a deserted farmhouse that the players used as their locker room.

Up to that point, the golfers who had played on both the Farwell estate and the sheep farm had been a loosely structured group. But in 1895 they officially organized and founded the Onwentsia Club, choosing for their name an Indian word that means "meeting spot for sporting braves and their squaws." One of their first acts was to purchase a larger local farm so they could build an eighteen-hole course. The first nine was constructed in 1896 and a second added in 1898. One hundred years later, there is still some confusion about who actually designed the course. In his book, *Scotland's Gift—Golf,* Macdonald gives credit to his son-in-law, Henry James Whigham. But other reference sources say that Macdonald laid out the first nine with help from the club professionals, Robert and James Foulis, and that Whigham, the Foulis brothers, and Herbert James Tweedie created the second loop. The finished product, which was originally planned as a typical British seaside course, measured just over 6,100 yards, and each hole had a colorful name; The Fool, Bonnie Bush, Isle of Woe, and Boomerang are just a few.

The U.S. Open came to Onwentsia just ten years after the first nine was put in, and the odds-on favorite was Willie Anderson. Not only had the Scottish ace won the last three championships in a row and four of the past five, but he was also working as the Onwentsia Club profes-

sional and knew the layout well. Victory seemed within Anderson's reach after fifty-four holes, and he was only three shots off the pace. But he fell apart in the final round, carding an eighty-four and finishing fifth, twelve strokes behind fellow Scotsman Alex Smith, who became the first golfer in Open history to shoot under three hundred for seventy-two holes. It was a good tournament for the entire Smith clan: Alex's brother, Willie, was runner-up, seven shots back; his brother-in-law James Maiden, came in third; and a third Smith brother, George, ended up tied for eighteenth. Although the Open might have been the biggest attraction at Onwentsia that weekend, it certainly wasn't the only one: polo teams from St. Louis and Kansas City played several matches during the Championship on a field encircled by the golf course.

Onwentsia has never hosted another Open. The course has undergone some changes over the years, but it remains more or less the same track that Alex Smith played so well in 1906. And the club continues to be the kind of spot its founders had in mind when they started up more than a century ago, a wonderful meeting place for sporting men and women.

ONWENTSIA CLUB'S SECOND INCARNATION WAS ON A FARM ABOUT THIRTY MILES NORTH OF CHICAGO. THE ABANDONED FARMHOUSE HERE WAS USED AS A CLUBHOUSE AND THE MAIN HAZARD WAS A LARGE FLOCK OF SHEEP. ONCE THE CLUB WAS OFFICIALLY FOUNDED IN 1895, IT MOVED TO ANOTHER FARM NEARBY, WHERE AN EIGHTEEN-HOLE COURSE WAS COMPLETED IN 1898. (ONWENTSIA CLUB)

Pebble Beach Golf Links

1972, 1982, 1992, 2000

JACK NICKLAUS TOOK THE 1972 OPEN BY THREE STROKES AFTER HIS FAMOUS ONE-IRON SHOT INTO THE OCEAN WIND HERE ON THE 209-YARD, PAR-THREE SEVENTEENTH. THE SHOT HIT THE PIN AND FELL SIX INCHES FROM THE HOLE.

(PEBBLE BEACH COMPANY)

Jack Nicklaus says it's his favorite. So does Tom Watson. "And not only because I won there," adds the Kansas City native. "There's just something special about it." Johnny Miller agrees, "It's the most beautiful place in the world, like it was made in heaven, and I can't think of another course I enjoy as much as Pebble Beach."

Who can? The 6,800-yard track that winds along Carmel Bay in northern California is rightfully regarded as one of the finest on earth. It was created by Samuel Morse, the nephew of the man who invented the telegraph. A sportsman who loved the natural beauty of the Monterey Peninsula, he bought seven thousand acres of land there in 1915, including seven miles of oceanfront property. His dream was to use part of that acreage for a golf resort, and he set aside his best parcels

for a course. Then he hired two of California's top amateur players, Jack Neville and Douglas Grant, to lay out his track. Neither man had ever designed a golf course before, but their knowledge of the game was strong. After only a few weeks of walking the dramatic land that Morse had designated for his resort, they came up with a plan.

The Pebble Beach Golf Links opened for play in 1918, and a professional named Mike Brady shot seventy-nine and seventy-five in an inaugural competition. But none of the other players came even close, and suddenly there were fears that the layout might be too difficult. Morse closed the course so Neville and Grant could soften it up and then reopened it for good on Washington's Birthday the next year. The par seventy-four course measured 6,314 yards at that time, and eight of its holes ran along the rocky shore.

Pebble Beach has been revised on a couple of occasions since then. H. Chandler Egan, Robert Hunter, and Roger Lapham worked on the track before it hosted the U.S. Amateur in 1929, remodeling several greens and bunkers and increasing the length some two hundred yards. They also changed the first hole to a dogleg right and transformed the eighteenth into the classic, par-five finishing hole it is today. More recently, in 1991, Jack Nicklaus headed a restoration effort that eradicated all kikuyu grass, reseeded the course with perennial rye, reconstructed several greens, and renovated a number of tees and bunkers.

PEBBLE BEACH, SEASIDE SITE OF THREE U.S. OPENS, IS THE ONLY PUBLIC COURSE TO HAVE HOSTED AN OPEN—PINEHURST WILL EARN THAT DISTINCTION IN 1999.
(LARRY LAMBRECHT)

PEBBLE BEACH'S SIXTH HOLE IS A 516-YARD PAR FIVE. THE COURSE'S OCEANSIDE LOCATION OFTEN PRODUCES DIFFICULT PLAYING CONDITIONS. TOM KITE FINALLY WON HIS FIRST MAJOR AT PEBBLE BEACH, BATTLING FOG AND FORTY-MILE-PER-HOUR WINDS DURING THE 1992 U.S. OPEN. (PEBBLE BEACH COMPANY)

The idea was not to make any radical changes to Pebble but rather to strengthen its impressive character and feel.

Pebble Beach hosted a number of national tournaments over the years, including three U.S. Amateurs and two Women's Amateurs. In addition, it was the venue for what is now called the AT&T Pro-Am. But, in spite of its great layout and impeccable reputation, the resort could not get a U.S. Open. The primary problem was location, and the United States Golf Association worried that attendance would be a concern at a course so far from a major metropolitan area. But the growing crowds at the annual Pro-Am, which was then known as the Crosby, eventually convinced the USGA that Pebble could bring in the fans, and the course was awarded the 1972 Open.

Nicklaus was the favorite that year, with good reason. For one thing, he knew the course and had played it well. He had won the '61

Amateur at Pebble, for example, and had captured two Crosbys as well. In addition, he was coming off his fourth win at the Masters. So no one was surprised when he took the lead with an opening-round seventy-one and stayed on top the entire four days. His seventy-two-hole score of 290 was the highest since World War II, but the course had played tough, especially on Sunday when the wind howled. Nicklaus clinched his victory on the par three seventeenth, hitting perhaps the most famous shot of his career, a one iron that hit the flagstick and settled six inches from the hole.

The seventeenth played a huge part in Tom Watson's only Open win ten years later. Leading after three rounds, he was locked in one of his famous duels with Nicklaus. The Golden Bear was playing three groups ahead of Watson and shot sixty-nine the last day to finish at 284. As he stepped to the sixteenth tee, Watson knew that all he needed to do was par the last three holes to win. But he immediately pushed his drive into a bunker and ended up with a bogey. Then his tee shot on the 209-yard seventeenth landed in the heavy greenside rough, and it looked like he was in deep trouble. With Nicklaus watching from a television monitor at the scorer's table, Watson took out his sand wedge and chipped in for a two. "As soon as it landed on the green I knew it was going in," he said afterward. "I just about jumped into the Pacific." Watson then birdied

THE SCENIC SEVENTH HOLE, A 107-YARD PAR THREE THAT JUTS OUT ON A PENINSULA, IS THE SECOND OF FIVE HOLES AT PEBBLE BEACH ARRANGED ALONG CARMEL BAY. (PEBBLE BEACH COMPANY)

eighteen to win by two. The first man to congratulate him as he walked off the green was Jack Nicklaus.

The 1992 Open belonged to Texan Tom Kite, who was known as both the all-time leading money winner on the PGA Tour and as the best golfer never to have won a major. Fortunately, he would soon be rid of that last label. Standing one stroke off the pace at the end of fifty-four holes, Kite battled strong winds and his own doubts to shoot a final-round seventy-two and take home the major that had eluded him for so long.

Although it was once shunned by the USGA, Pebble Beach is now an important part of the Open rotation and will host the championship again in the year 2000. Nicklaus, Watson, and Miller may not be playing in that event, but the field will be full of other professionals who think that Samuel Morse's course on Carmel Bay is one of the best things ever to happen to golf. Pebble Beach is just that good.

The Philadelphia Country Club

1939

This championship is best remembered as the Open that Sam Snead lost to Byron Nelson, and it took place on the Spring Mill course in 1939. Designed by William Flynn and Howard Toomey, the course opened in 1927 and was remodeled by Percy Maxwell the year before the Open came to town.

Golf had been a part of the Philadelphia Country Club long before that tournament was played, however. Members started fooling around with the game in 1891, the year after the club's founding. "Golf was then being played on Long Island, and although it appeared to us as a game very nearly related to croquet, we thought it might furnish mild amusement and determined to give it a tryout," explained member H.C. Groome, Jr. in an interview that was reprinted in the club's centennial history. "Three empty cans (which according to their labels formerly held French peas) were inserted in the lawn in a triangle, the sides of which measured about 75 yards; clubs were sent for, and every stray Englishman who appeared at the club was immediately impressed as an expounder of the 'ancient and honorable' game." A nine-hole course was built the following year, and in 1894 the club held its first tournament. Three years later the members added another nine.

This game very nearly related to croquet became wildly popular at the Philadelphia Country Club, so much so that the club eventually had to institute starting times. Overcrowding had become such a problem that in 1924 the club decided to buy 210 acres of nearby land and build a new golf course, which it called Spring Mill.

As it was set up for the 1939 Open, Spring Mill had a par of sixty-nine, the lowest ever for an Open, and it measured 6,786 yards. Only one of the holes was a par five for the event—the 555-yard eighteenth—while two holes that played as par fives for members—the 479-yard eighth and the 480-yard twelfth - were designated par fours. "Some of the holes were awfully long," says eventual champion Nelson, "and that made the whole course tough. The average score was two over par."

It was a spectacular tournament. Sam Snead had been the hottest golfer on the Tour that year, and he started the final round one stroke off the pace. Standing on the seventeenth tee that day, he needed only a pair of pars for a seventy and a four-round total of 282, which would have been good enough to beat Nelson, who had just finished with a

WHEN THE PHILADELPHIA COUNTRY CLUB HOSTED THE 1939 OPEN ON ITS 6,786-YARD SPRING MILL COURSE, PAR WAS LOWERED TO SIXTY-NINE—THE LOWEST EVER IN AN OPEN. THE 555-YARD EIGHTEENTH WAS THE ONLY PAR FIVE OF THE CHAMPIONSHIP. (USGA)

Byron Nelson labored through two eighteen-hole play-offs on the lengthy Spring Mill Course at Philadelphia before he edged out Craig Wood by three. (USGA)

sixty-eight for 284. Even when Snead bogeyed the seventeenth, his lead seemed safe—until he fell apart on eighteen. After hooking his drive into the rough, he topped a two wood into a bunker one hundred yards from the green. His ball plugged into the sand, and it took him two shots to get out. He put his fourth into another bunker and, after blasting onto the green, three-putted for an eight. Snead ended up two strokes off the lead, behind Nelson and two others, Craig Wood and Denny Shute. Those three met in a play-off the following day. Shute was eliminated when he shot a seventy-six, but Wood and Nelson both carded sixty-eights and remained tied. Tournament officials asked the pros if they wanted to settle the title in sudden death, but they insisted on another eighteen-hole play-off. So they went at it again on Tuesday. Nelson eagled the fourth when he holed out a one iron from 215 yards and finished with a seventy to win by three strokes.

Philadelphia Cricket Club

1907, 1910

The Philadelphia Cricket Club was started in 1854 by a group of University of Pennsylvania students looking for a way to continue playing their favorite sport after they graduated from college. And it remained the club's primary focus for the next three decades. But in time, its members got involved in other games. Tennis became a popular recreation, for example, and the club helped found the American Lawn Tennis Association. Horseback riding also developed into an appealing pastime, and for many years the renowned Philadelphia Horse Show was held on Cricket Club grounds. Golf, too, interested the members, and in

ALEX ROSS, BROTHER OF FAMED COURSE DESIGNER DONALD ROSS, WON THE 1907 OPEN HERE AT THE PHILADELPHIA CRICKET CLUB WITH A 302. (COUNTRY CLUB MAGAZINE)

ALEX SMITH BEAT HIS YOUNGER
BROTHER MACDONALD SMITH AND
JOHN MCDERMOTT IN A PLAY-OFF TO
CLAIM THE 1910 OPEN TITLE AT THE
PHILADELPHIA CRICKET CLUB. (COUNTRY
CLUB MAGAZINE)

1895 they built a nine-hole course on some land in the St. Martin's section of Chestnut Hill. Two years later they constructed a new eighteen-hole track, which had been designed by a committee of members. It was a fine layout that went on to host two national championships.

The first Open came to the Cricket Club in 1907 in the midst of some brutally hot and humid weather. Alex Ross—whose older brother, Donald, went on to design some of the country's best courses—led by a shot after the first day, going seventy-six and seventy-four. He fell to third after carding a seventy-six the second morning of the tournament but came back to win by two strokes as his closest competitors wilted in the heat. One of those was Jack Hobens, who had the lead after three rounds, thanks in part to his recording the first hole-in-one in Open history on the 147-yard tenth. But he staggered to an eighty-five for the final eighteen and finished fourth, seven shots back. Another player who let the weather get the better of him was A.W. Tillinghast, a talented player who would later make his mark as a course architect; he was low amateur coming into the thirteenth hole on the last round but was overcome by heat and forced to withdraw.

The Open returned to the Cricket Club three years later. The par seventy-three St. Martin's course measured 5,956 yards, and more than seventy competitors started the first day. Alex Smith carded a pair of seventy-threes to take a two-stroke lead, but he struggled to a seventy-nine in the third round and ended up tied at the end of seventy-two holes with his younger brother, Macdonald, and Philadelphian John McDermott. The three met in a play-off the following day, and Alex Smith prevailed, posting a seventy-one to McDermott's seventy-five and his brother's seventy-seven.

It has been years since cricket was played at the club, but members still love their golf. Unfortunately, they don't get to play the old Open course anymore. At least not all of it. The original track, it seems, was built on land the club didn't own, and when the family who held the deed said they wouldn't sell, the members purchased a large piece of property in nearby Flourtown and constructed a new eighteen-hole course. The old St. Martin's course was reduced to a nine-holer in 1925 as most of the golfing activity moved to the new layout. But it remains a fun place to play, and even though it's only nine holes, St. Martin's still gives golfers a sense of the course on which Ross and Smith won their titles because the first, second, eighth, and ninth holes have hardly changed in ninety years.

Pinehurst Resort and Country Club

1999

It was completed in 1907 and has long been regarded as one of the best tracks in the world. Yet No. 2 at the Pinehurst Resort and Country Club has had to wait all these years to host a U.S. Open. But as the saying goes, better late than never.

The story of Pinehurst begins in the late 1800s when a Bostonian named James Walker Tufts traveled to North Carolina in hopes of building a warm-weather resort for New Englanders. After surveying several locations, he bought five thousand acres of cut-over timberland from the Page family of Aberdeen. The price: one dollar an acre. Shortly thereafter, Tufts built a small hotel, a store, several boardinghouses, and a handful of cottages. On New Year's Day 1901 he opened the spacious Carolina Hotel, which was to become the cornerstone of the Pinehurst Resort.

THE PGA BROUGHT ITS CHAMPIONSHIP TO PINEHURST ONLY A YEAR AFTER COURSE DESIGNER DONALD ROSS REPLACED SAND GREENS WITH GRASS IN 1935. IN 1999 PINEHURST WILL BECOME ONE OF ONLY EIGHTEEN COURSES TO HAVE HOSTED BOTH THE PGA CHAMPIONSHIP AND THE U.S. OPEN.
(PINEHURST RESORT AND COUNTRY CLUB)

Tufts wanted sports to be an important part of the Pinehurst experience, but he hadn't thought of including golf until he received an angry call from a neighboring dairy farmer complaining that his guests were swatting little white balls with odd-looking sticks into his pasture and frightening his cows. Rather than chastising his guests, Tufts decided to accommodate them. He asked an amateur designer from New York, Dr. LeRoy Culver, to lay out a nine-hole golf course. Nine more holes were added in 1899, and Pinehurst No. 1 was born. Harry Vardon visited the resort the following year and was impressed with the course.

"It is very sporty, no two holes being alike, the distances are excellent and the hazards are well placed," he wrote in a letter to Tufts after his visit. "You will have eighteen holes which will be a great pleasure for any golfer to play over."

The next year Tufts hired a full-time professional, a Scotsman named Donald Ross, to serve as his director of golf. A keen player and former greenskeeper who had been apprenticed to Old Tom Morris at St. Andrews and designed several courses in the Boston area, Ross quickly revamped the first course and began building another, which would come to be known as No. 2. Ross stayed at Pinehurst for forty-eight years, and although he would go on to design two other courses at the resort and many others of great repute throughout the United States, No. 2 is regarded as perhaps his greatest creation. The par seventy-two, 7,020-yard track boasts small, sloping greens that play even smaller because they fall off all around the edges, deep bunkers, loose sandy soil, Pencross bentgrass greens and Bermuda rough accented by native wiregrass. Raymond Floyd calls it "truly magnificent," and Sam Snead rates it his "number one course." The major golf magazines think highly of it as well: No. 2 was ninth on *Golf Digest's* 1995 list of America's 100 Greatest Golf Courses and sixth on *Golf Magazine's*.

Although this will be its first Open, Pinehurst No. 2 has hosted major tournaments before; the 1936 PGA Championship was played there after its sand greens were replaced with grass, as were the 1951

THE CAROLINA HOTEL, OPENED NEW YEAR'S DAY 1901, IS THE CENTERPIECE OF THE LUXURIOUS RESORT AT PINEHURST. FAMED COURSE DESIGNER DONALD ROSS BECAME HEAD GOLF PROFESSIONAL AT THE CLUB THE NEXT YEAR, A POSITION HE HELD FOR FORTY-EIGHT YEARS. (PINEHURST RESORT AND COUNTRY CLUB)

Ryder Cup, the 1962 U.S. Amateur, and the 1994 U.S. Senior Open. It was also the site of Ben Hogan's first professional tournament win, in the North and South Open, after seven frustrating years on the Tour.

Riviera Country Club

1948

IN 1948, BEN HOGAN WON HIS SECOND CONSECUTIVE LOS ANGELES OPEN AT RIVIERA. THAT SUMMER HE CAPTURED THE U.S. OPEN TITLE THERE AS WELL, EARNING THE COURSE THE NICKNAME "HOGAN'S ALLEY." (RIVIERA COUNTRY CLUB)

Stand on one of the clubhouse verandas at the Riviera Country Club in Los Angeles today and imagine what Frank Garbutt must have seen some seventy-five years ago as he gazed out from the bluff on which the majestic building now stands and into the Santa Monica Canyon below. The vice president of the Los Angeles Athletic Club, he was looking for a place to build a golf course for his members. At first glance the canyon seemed an inappropriate spot, with all the brush and trees tangled into

an unwieldy mass. But Garbutt recognized its potential immediately, exclaiming, "This is it! This is it!" as he marveled at the property below.

Some time later, Garbutt brought architect George Thomas to the same vista and asked if he would be able to carve a quality golf course out of that land. A wealthy Philadelphia native who had already designed tracks at the Los Angeles and Bel Air Country Clubs, Thomas thoughtfully surveyed the canyon and offered the following opinion: He could build a course there, but it would cost plenty. That was fine with Garbutt, and Thomas went to work.

It was an extraordinary undertaking. A crew of more than two hundred men spent the next year and a half clearing the canyon, installing one hundred thousand feet of pipe for a sprinkling system, spreading topsoil that had been trucked in from the San Fernando Valley, planting nineteen thousand pounds of grass seed, and adding more than thirteen hundred tons of beach sand. The final price tag came to an astounding

WHEN FRANK GARBUTT COMMISSIONED GEORGE THOMAS TO BUILD RIVIERA IN 1922, HE TOLD HIM TO SPARE NO EXPENSE. THE RESULT WAS A MAJESTIC COURSE THAT COST $650,000—SIX TIMES MORE THAN THE AVERAGE COURSE AT THE TIME. (RIVIERA COUNTRY CLUB)

THE ELEGANT AND GLAMOROUS RIVIERA
COUNTRY CLUB HAS CLAIMED A NUMBER
OF WELL-KNOWN MEMBERS THROUGH
THE YEARS, INCLUDING MARY PICKFORD,
GREGORY PECK, KATHARINE HEPBURN,
AND SPENCER TRACY. (MIKE KLEMME/GOLFOTO)

$650,000, more than six times what it cost to build an average course in those days. Despite the exorbitant price tag, Thomas had created one of the finest layouts in the land. In fact, the National Golf Foundation immediately ranked Riviera third on a list of the world's top ten courses, behind Pine Valley and Pinehurst No. 2. It opened in June 1927 and featured a number of interesting design twists. The par-three sixth hole had a bunker in the middle of the green that made it look like a doughnut, for example, while the par-four eighth boasted alternate fairways.

As might be expected from a club located in Los Angeles, the membership roll at Riviera has included some glamorous names over the years, such as Douglas Fairbanks, Dean Martin, Gregory Peck, W.C. Fields, Spencer Tracy, Katharine Hepburn, James Garner, Mary Pickford, Glen Campbell, Robert Wagner, and Burt Lancaster. It has also been the site of some memorable tournaments. In 1929 Riviera hosted the Los Angeles Open for the first time, and the event, which is now dubbed the Nissan Open, has been played there ever since. It wasn't until 1948, however, that the club held its first and only U.S. Open.

The fastest player out of the gate that year was Sam Snead, who was still searching for his first national championship. Snead had lost the 1947 Open at St. Louis in a play-off with Lew Worsham, and he seemed more determined than ever when he arrived at Riviera, carding a pair of sixty-nines to lead by a stroke over Ben Hogan and South African Bobby Locke. Sadly, Snead again faded on the final day, shooting rounds of seventy-three and seventy-two and finishing fifth with a seventy-two-hole score of 283. But Hogan rose to the occasion, posting sixty-eight and sixty-nine on Saturday for a record 276 and a two-stroke win over Jimmy Demaret. It was the first of four Open wins for the Hawk and came about a month after he had taken the PGA Championship. It was also the third time he had won at Riviera in less than eighteen months, having captured the 1947 and 1948 Los Angeles Open titles as well. From that point on, the course that George Thomas built in that scruffy canyon has been known as Hogan's Alley.

Scioto Country Club

1926

Two of the greatest names in golf come to mind whenever the Scioto Country Club is mentioned: Bobby Jones and Jack Nicklaus. Jones won the U.S. Open when it was held at the Columbus, Ohio, club in 1926, and Nicklaus learned to play golf there. Another famous name associated with the club is Samuel P. Bush. A local steel industry executive, he was one of the men who founded Scioto. He also happens to be the grandfather of the forty-first president of the United States.

The story of Scioto actually began in the clubhouse at the National Golf Links in Southampton, Long Island, where Bush was relaxing after a round in the spring of 1913 with three other Ohio residents, James Hamill, W.K. Lanman, and Buster Sheldon. They were all lamenting the absence of an eighteen-hole course in Columbus when they hit on the idea of building one of their own. A year later they bought thirty acres of farmland and signed an option to purchase 165 more. That done, the men began assembling a roll of prospective members and looking for a course architect. A number of different designers were considered, but the club's first president, James Hamill, opted for one of the best, Donald Ross. Hamill visited Ross at his residence in Pinehurst, North Carolina, and offered him seventy-five dollars a day, plus expenses, to map out a plan. Ross came up with a suitable design, and the Scioto board hired him for the job.

The track was completed in the summer of 1916, and the first round was played on July 1 that year, with Hamill and Bush part of the inaugural foursome. Ten years later an even headier group of golfers teed it up

when Scioto hosted the 1926 U.S. Open. Not surprisingly the pretournament favorite was Bobby Jones, who had just won his first British Open
title, and that sentiment seemed justified after he carded a two-under-par
seventy for his opening round. The championship was being held for the
first time over three days, not two, and perhaps the extra time between
rounds bothered Jones because he shot a seventy-nine on the second day,
his highest score ever in an Open. But Scioto was not playing easy for
anybody that week, mainly because the rough had been allowed to grow
up so high. Jock Hutchison, for example, said he was competing in "a little money match" the day before the Open began when he drove his ball
into the rough. When he couldn't find it, his opponents told him to drop
another, which he did and promptly lost. "And while I was looking for
that ball," he said afterward, "I lost my caddie."

The rough didn't seem to bother Jones on Saturday. He shot
seventy-one in the morning and entered the final round three back of
the leader, Joe Turnesa. The son of a Westchester County, New York
greenskeeper, Turnesa added a stroke to his lead after posting a thirty-
seven on the front to Jones's thirty-eight, and when both men parred

DONALD ROSS'S TIGHT, UNDULATING
GREENS FACTOR AS HEAVILY INTO A
ROUND OF GOLF AT SCIOTO TODAY AS
THEY DID IN THE 1926 OPEN. (PAT SEELIG)

ten and eleven, Jones found himself four back with seven to play. But he hit the ball brilliantly the rest of the way, while Turnesa fell apart, limping home with a seventy-seven. When Jones stepped to the tee of the par five eighteenth, he knew he was tied for the lead and needed only a birdie to win. True to form, he hit a mammoth drive and then stroked a mashie to within fifteen feet. After two putts, he was Open champion again.

Obviously, Jack Nicklaus hadn't even been born when Jones sealed his Open win. But his father, Charlie, who was a sixteen-year-old drug-store clerk at the time, was there that day. Some 25 years later he was working in his own drugstore when Scioto's new pro, Jack Grout, stopped by to fill a prescription. The elder Nicklaus, who was a member of the club, introduced himself and said he had heard Grout was starting a junior golf class. He told Grout about his nine-year-old son, Jack, and asked if there might be room for him in the class. Grout told him there was, and the rest, as they say, is history.

Scioto never had another Open, but the club has hosted several other major events, including the 1931 Ryder Cup, the 1950 PGA Championship, the 1968 U.S. Amateur and the 1986 Senior Open. Although the members loved their Donald Ross track, they decided after much debate in the early 1960s to modernize the layout and brought in architect Dick Wilson to handle the task. He made plenty of changes but was careful to make sure the course didn't lose any of its character.

Shinnecock Hills Golf Club

1896, 1986, 1995

The Shinnecock Hills Golf Club has been based in the tiny Long Island town of Southampton since the fall of 1891, but its roots go back even further. William K. Vanderbilt was vacationing on the Bay of Biscay in southwestern France the winter before with two of his friends, Duncan

SHINNECOCK HILLS GOLF CLUB BOASTS THE FIRST CLUBHOUSE IN THE UNITED STATES. DESIGNED BY RENOWNED NEW YORK ARCHITECT STANFORD WHITE, IT OPENED IN 1892. (USGA)

Cryder and Edward Mead, when they met the Scottish golfing great Willie Dunn, who was designing a course for the nearby spa at Biarritz. Dunn gave the Americans an impromptu demonstration of the strange, new game, and they were all intrigued by what they saw. Shortly afterward, Cryder wrote to his friend Samuel Parrish and suggested that they try and introduce the sport in Southampton, where both of them were part-time residents.

Parrish liked the idea, and that summer he had another Scotsman, Willie Davis, build a twelve-hole course there. It took three months to construct it with the help of 150 Native Americans from the Shinnecock tribe who lived on a nearby reservation. The club was incorporated on September 21, 1891, making it the first official golf club in America. By the following June Shinnecock also had the first clubhouse in the country, a white-shingled country house designed by Stanford White, the famed New York architect who counted Madison Square Garden and

SHINNECOCK HOSTED THE SECOND OPEN, HELD IN 1896; THE TOURNAMENT DIDN'T RETURN UNTIL 1986, WHEN RAYMOND FLOYD CAPTURED HIS FIRST OPEN TITLE. (ROBERT WALKER)

Penn Station among his works. Some time later a nine-hole women's track was added, but the club eventually combined those two courses into one eighteen-hole layout measuring 4,423 yards. The architect of this consolidation was the club professional and the man who had helped start it all, Willie Dunn.

In 1894 Shinnecock joined four other golf clubs in founding the United States Golf Association and two years later hosted the second U.S. Open. The early money pegged two-time British Open champion Willie Park, Jr. as the favorite, but he wasn't able to play; his boat was late in crossing the Atlantic and didn't dock until the day after the tournament was over. The title was won instead by James Foulis, the pro from the Chicago Golf Club, whose rounds of seventy-eight and seventy-four were good enough to beat the winner of the inaugural Open, Horace Rawlings, by three strokes. The field included a former Shinnecock caddie of African-American descent named John Shippen,

SHINNECOCK DESIGNER WILLIE DAVIS USED THE HILLY LANDSCAPE OF LONG ISLAND TO CREATE A COURSE CLOSELY AKIN TO THE LINKS COURSES OF HIS HOMELAND. ALTHOUGH THE ORIGINAL COURSE WAS ABANDONED IN 1928 FOR A NEW COURSE DESIGNED BY WILLIAM FLYNN, THE LANDSCAPE AND THE TREACHEROUS CLUSTERS OF BUNKERS PRESERVE THE LINKS FEEL. (ROBERT WALKER)

who finished tied for sixth, seven strokes back. Shippen won ten dollars for his efforts, and there's no telling how much more he could have earned if he hadn't posted an eleven on the thirteenth hole during his second and final round. Another competitor of note was Oscar Bunn, a full-blooded Shinnecock who had also worked as a caddie at the club. He came in twenty-first.

Many of the twenty-eight players who completed both rounds at the 1896 Open scored in the seventies, and that prompted the club to lengthen its course by a thousand yards soon after. An even longer championship track was created in 1901, and it lasted until Suffolk County decided to extend a major highway directly through the club grounds in 1928. Shinnecock solved the problem by buying some adjoining land and building a new course. Designed by William Flynn and opened in 1930, it was a wonderfully rugged, links-style track with tall rough and windswept sandhills.

From its reopening, Shinnecock was revered among golfers as one of the best courses in the country. But the site of a U.S. Open? It didn't seem possible. For one thing, Shinnecock was located in a fairly remote area, and only one road ran to and from the club. In addition, it had a reasonably small membership and couldn't offer the sort of volunteer help a major championship required. Still, the USGA could not ignore the history and quality of the course itself, and finally decided to send the 1986 Open out to Southampton.

It was a good choice. The players raved about the track, and there were none of the anticipated traffic problems. Although it wasn't the financial success of past championships, the Shinnecock Open provided a wealth of drama. Greg Norman led after fifty-four holes, but several competitors made a run at the championship the final afternoon, and at one point eight men were tied for the lead: Lee Trevino, Hal Sutton, Bob Tway, Mark McCumber, Lanny Wadkins, Chip Beck, Payne Stewart, and Norman. None of them would win, however, because Ray Floyd came charging out of the pack to shoot sixty-six and take his first Open title.

That tournament went so well that the USGA returned in 1995. Again, Greg Norman had the lead after fifty-four holes, and again he lost it, this time to Corey Pavin, who stepped to the eighteenth tee with a one-shot advantage over the Shark. The finishing hole at Shinnecock is one of golf's finest, 450 yards long with the last two hundred yards heading straight uphill to a smallish green. Pavin is not one of the game's biggest hitters, and his drive left him more than two hundred yards from the pin. He thought about using a two iron but grabbed his four wood instead and hit the shot of his life, the ball coming to rest five feet from the flag. Pavin missed his birdie putt, but still hung on for the win.

The USGA hasn't said when it will go back to Shinnecock, but as far as most Tour players are concerned, it won't be soon enough. Says Johnny Miller, the 1973 Open champ and NBC golf commentator, "Pebble Beach is my all-time favorite, but Shinnecock is a close second. If I had my way, the Open would alternate between those two courses—Pebble and Shinnecock, Shinnecock and Pebble—and maybe go to a Medinah or an Oakmont every fifth year. Shinnecock is just that good."

Skokie Country Club

1922

"Change" is the first word that comes to mind when one thinks of the Skokie Country Club in Glencoe, Illinois. The course there has had more face lifts than a Hollywood starlet. The original version was a nine-holer built in 1898 by member George Leslie. Working with seventy-five acres of land and a budget of just over $1,500, he created a 3,061-yard layout that was described in a club brochure as "sporty."

It may have well been that, but the members soon wanted more, and in 1904 they decided to build a full eighteen-hole track. They acquired some additional land and hired the Scottish architect Tom Bendelow. He constructed a 6,125-yard course that opened the following year to mixed reviews. *American Golfer* described the greens as the "best in the West." But the members didn't like some aspects of the new design, and in 1914 they asked Donald Ross to give it a makeover. The course he created was vastly different from what had been there before.

It was also better, and eight years later Skokie hosted the 1922 U.S. Open. Walter Hagen shot a sixty-eight to head the field after the first

ALTHOUGH BOBBY JONES PUTTED ADMIRABLY AT THE 1922 OPEN AT SKOKIE, IT WAS NOT ENOUGH TO BEAT OPPONENT GENE SARAZEN. JONES LOST TO SARAZEN BY ONE, FINISHING IN A TIE FOR SECOND WITH JOHN BLACK AT 289. (SKOKIE COUNTRY CLUB)

round, but he fell back a bit after carding a seventy-seven in round two. Bobby Jones had the hot hand the next morning, posting a seventy to tie for the third-round lead with Wild Bill Mehlhorn. But the final eighteen—and the tournament—would belong to Gene Sarazen, a cocky twenty-year-old who had grown up playing on a public course in Bridgeport, Connecticut. Starting the final round four strokes back, he shot a one-under-par thirty-three on the front nine and then played the first eight holes of the back nine even. As he walked to the eighteenth tee, Sarazan calculated that he needed only to par the last hole for a sixty-nine and a seventy-two-hole score of 289 to win. He split the fairway with a long drive on the par five, but when he found that he had a good lie, he reached again for his driver and crushed his ball, putting it some fifteen feet from the pin. Two putts later he had his birdie and a sixty-eight, which put him at 288. It was a good thing, too, because his math had been wrong. Bobby Jones and a Scottish immigrant named John Black had both ended up with 289s; Sarazen's four on eighteen was the difference.

DESIGNED ORIGINALLY BY GEORGE LESLIE IN 1898 WITH THE SECOND NINE ADDED BY TOM BENDELOW IN 1904, THE COURSE AT SKOKIE WAS REVAMPED TO ITS PRESENT FORM BY DONALD ROSS IN 1915. (SKOKIE COUNTRY CLUB)

You would have thought that after their club had hosted an Open the members of Skokie would have left well enough alone. But complacency seemed a crime to them. They acquired some additional property in the late 1930s and brought in architect William Langford to tinker even further with their layout. A former member of the Yale golf team, Langford had completed his engineering studies at MIT and apprenticed for Tom Bendelow. He described what he was doing as a "rearrangement," but it seemed that he did much more. When all was finished Langford had put in eight new holes at a cost of $38,000.

It was thirty years before the club did any significant work on the course again. The architect this time was Rees Jones, and he planted trees, added bunkers, redesigned tees, and put in a new green or two. In 1993 three more greens were torn up and rebuilt, and the pond on the third hole was renovated. Nothing much has happened since, but it surely won't be long before the members get in the mood for another change.

Southern Hills Country Club

1958, 1977, 2001

It was during the depths of the Great Depression when rumors started circulating that the Tulsa Country Club was about to close because of financial problems. Several members approached oilman Waite Phillips and asked for his help in building another golf course. Phillips said he would give them some land, but only if they could raise $150,000 within a couple of weeks and agree to construct a true country club with facilities for swimming, tennis, and other recreational activities in addition to golf. The money was quickly raised, and Percy Maxwell was hired to build the course. It was completed in 1936, a 6,900-yard, par seventy track that became the centerpiece of a new club known as Southern Hills.

Southern Hills was considered a championship course right from the start, but it didn't host its first U.S. Open until 1958. Dubbed the Blast Furnace Open because temperatures hovered around the one

hundred-degree mark all week, it also became famous for its slick greens, thick rough, and high scores. Gene Sarazen opened with eighty-four and eighty, and Sam Snead missed the Open cut for the first time in eighteen years when he shot seventy-five and eighty. Ben Hogan injured his wrist trying to power a ball out of the rough during a practice round, and the average score for the first day was an astounding seventy-nine. Not one competitor shot par or better.

Three players did turn in seventy-ones to share the first-round lead. One of them was forty-year-old Tommy Bolt, the tempestuous Oklahoman who seemed to be playing with new-found tranquility. He shot another seventy-one the second day and then posted sixty-nine

BECAUSE OF THE CONSTANT 100-DEGREE TEMPERATURES DURING THE 1958 OPEN AT SOUTHERN HILLS COUNTRY CLUB—WHICH HAS HOSTED MORE MAJOR COMPETITIONS THAN ANY OTHER COURSE IN THE SOUTH—THE EVENT WAS DUBBED THE BLAST FURNACE OPEN. ALTHOUGH NATIVE OKLAHOMAN TOMMY BOLT FINISHED THREE OVER PAR, HE STILL MANAGED TO COME OUT ON TOP BY FOUR STROKES. (SOUTHERN HILLS COUNTRY CLUB)

NARROW, TREE-LINED FAIRWAYS AND BALL-GRABBING BERMUDA GRASS MAKE SOUTHERN HILLS A CHALLENGING CHAMPIONSHIP COURSE. (SOUTHERN HILLS COUNTRY CLUB)

and seventy-two on Saturday for a seventy-two-hole score of 283 and his only major win. Four strokes back in sole possession of second place was twenty-two-year-old Gary Player, who was competing in his first U.S. Open. Julius Boros came in third and Gene Littler fourth.

It was nineteen years before Southern Hills hosted another Open, and the big story at that tournament was the death threat against Hubert Green. Green had led from the start, shooting sixty-nine on the first day, sixty-seven on the second, and seventy-two on the third. His

fifty-four-hole total came to 208 and left him one up on Andy Bean and two strokes ahead of six other golfers, including Tom Weiskopf and Gary Player. He continued his steady play on Sunday, carding a one-under-par thirty-four for the front nine, bogeying ten, and then parring the next four holes in a row. But as he walked off the green at fourteen, he was approached by United States Golf Association vice president Sandy Tatum, who told Green that a threat had been made on his life and asked him whether he wanted to withdraw, suspend play, or

DESPITE RUMORS THAT POLICE HAD RECEIVED A THREAT ON HIS LIFE, HUBERT GREEN MANAGED PAR OR BETTER FROM HOLES ELEVEN TO SEVENTEEN, PICTURED HERE, IN THE FINAL ROUND OF THE 1977 OPEN AT SOUTHERN HILLS. A BOGEY ON EIGHTEEN WAS STILL GOOD ENOUGH FOR THE WIN. (SOUTHERN HILLS COUNTRY CLUB)

continue. Green chose to continue, even joking that the threat had probably come from an old girlfriend. Accompanied by a phalanx of guards, he played the last four holes even par, making a courageous four-foot putt on eighteen for a one-stroke victory.

In spite of what its name might suggest, Southern Hills is basically a flat course. It is also long and tight, with fairways running through narrow corridors of trees. The greens are steeply banked from front to back, and if approach shots aren't positioned properly, three-putts are almost inevitable. Of all its holes, perhaps the most famous is the 456-yard twelfth, which Ben Hogan called the greatest par-four twelfth in America and Arnold Palmer included it in a book on his fifty-four favorite holes. It is a dogleg left that requires a superb drive and an accurate second shot to a green guarded by water to the front and right and bunkers to the back and left.

The Open, which will be returning to Tulsa in 2001, has been just one of several national tournaments that Southern Hills has hosted over the years. Babe Zaharias won the Women's Amateur there in 1946, and the PGA Championship was played there in 1970, 1982 and 1994. In addition, the club has hosted the Junior Amateur, the Senior Amateur, the Women's Mid-Amateur, and the U.S. Amateur.

St. Louis Country Club

1947

The St. Louis Country Club was organized in 1892. There were only fifteen charter members, and they used the old Collier farm in Bridgeton as their clubhouse and grounds. The membership roll grew rapidly over the next few years, and in 1895 the club decided to relocate to nearby Clayton, where a new clubhouse was constructed. Nineteen years later, the group moved again, settling in its present spot in Ladue, about ten miles west of the city center.

Golf was a popular recreation among members in the early days, and they had a wonderful course that had been designed by Charles Blair Macdonald. It was the site of the U.S. Amateur in 1921 and then

the Women's Amateur four years later. In 1947 the United States Golf Association held its national championship there.

The par seventy-one course was, at 6,532 yards, short for a U.S. Open track. The layout at Canterbury the previous year, for example, was about four hundred yards longer, while Colonial—site of the 1941 Open, which was the last one played before the tournament was suspended during World War II—measured more than seven thousand yards. But St. Louis seemed to play bigger than it was, and the average score was a respectable 75.8. Still, some of the players beat it up pretty good. Chick Harbert, Harry Todd, and Henry Ransom all carded sixty-sevens on the first day, while a group of four others posted sixty-eights. Harbert was still on top after thirty-six holes, having shot seventy-two on Friday for a two-round total of 139. He was joined by Dick Metz, with Lew Worsham a stroke back at 140. The big news Saturday morning was the sizzling sixty-five posted by amateur James McHale. It was, at the time, the lowest round in Open history, but it didn't put McHale atop the leader board. That position belonged to Worsham, a twenty-nine-year-old Virginia pro who

DURING THE 1947 U.S. OPEN AT ST. LOUIS, SAM SNEAD SUNK AN EIGHTEEN-FOOT PUTT ON THE 419-YARD, PAR-FOUR EIGHTEENTH TO FORCE A PLAY-OFF WITH LEW WORSHAM. WORSHAM EDGED OUT SNEAD BY A STROKE IN THE TIEBREAKER AFTER SNEAD MISSED A PUTT OF LESS THAN A YARD. (STEVE SPRAY)

stood in first place with a fifty-four-hole score of 211 and a one-stroke advantage over Sam Snead and Bobby Locke.

Snead had played well all week, following an opening round seventy-two with a pair of seventies. But when he went out for the final round Saturday afternoon, he promptly bogeyed the first two holes, and it looked like he was about to have one of his patented Open collapses. But he pulled himself together and played solidly the rest of the way, posting birdies at five, six and fifteen. He did bogey seventeen, and it looked for a moment like he would come up short in regulation again. But he drained a brilliant eighteen-foot birdie putt on eighteen to force a play-off with Worsham.

The next day's round provided great theater. Snead went out in thirty-four and held a one-stroke lead after nine. Worsham pulled even with a birdie at twelve, but Snead went ahead by two when he birdied twelve himself and then fifteen. But Worsham carded a two at sixteen to narrow the gap to one. And when Snead bogeyed seventeen, Worsham was back to even going into the final hole.

Snead put his second shot some twenty feet from the pin on eighteen, but Worsham's approach skidded off the back of the green. He almost holed his chip, running his shot three feet past. Snead left his first putt short, and he walked immediately to his ball to set up again. But Worsham called out, "Are you sure you're away?" He had the easier putt and wanted to put more pressure on Snead by making his first.

THE WATER ON ST. LOUIS'S THIRD HOLE IS EASILY CARRIED OFF THE TEE. A 6,532-YARD PAR SEVENTY-ONE, THE COURSE IS ONE OF THE SHORTEST TO HAVE HOSTED AN OPEN SINCE WORLD WAR II. (STEVE SPRAY)

Clearly irritated, Snead asked for a USGA official, insisting he had the right to play. A tape measure was brought in, and it showed that Snead was out by about an inch. So he set up again. But he tapped his ball too lightly, and it fell away at the last minute, stopping a couple of inches outside the hole. Worsham walked calmly to his ball and stroked it in for par, giving him a 69 and a one-shot win.

St. Louis has never hosted another U.S. Open and chances are it never will because the layout simply isn't long or difficult enough for the pros anymore. But it was the site of the 1960 U.S. Amateur, which was won by future PGA commissioner Deane Beman, and in 1972 it hosted the Women's Amateur for the second time.

The Country Club

1913, 1963, 1988

Everything about The Country Club seems to be steeped in history. The town in which it is located—Brookline, Massachusetts—was settled in 1634, just fourteen years after the Pilgrims landed at Plymouth Rock. The club itself was founded in the early 1880s as a place for Boston Brahmins to gather for tennis, lawn bowling, horseback riding, and other forms of recreation. Golf didn't come into the picture until the early 1890s when a Frenchwoman named Florence Boit came to visit her uncle, Arthur Hunnewell, at his Brookline estate. She had brought along her golf clubs, and because there were no courses in the area, Boit hit balls into flower pots she had arranged on the lawn. A neighbor named Laurence Curtis watched that strange spectacle for a while and then wrote a letter to The Country Club, asking if golf could be introduced. After a long debate, the board said yes and gave Curtis permission to build a course. A six-hole track was quickly constructed, and not long afterward it was expanded to nine holes by Willie Campbell.

The game caught on quickly, and Brookline became a major part of its development in America, joining four other clubs in 1894 to form what is known today as the United States Golf Association. By the turn of the century the course had grown to eighteen holes, and in 1913 it hosted its first U.S. Open. The big favorites were two British players,

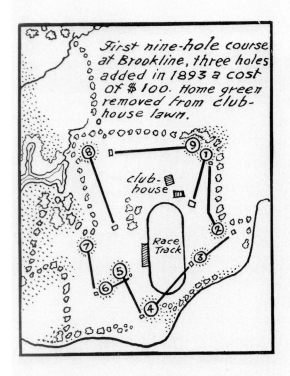

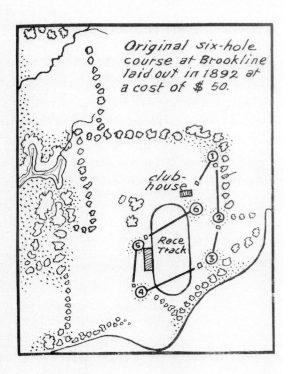

Harry Vardon and Ted Ray, and true to form they led the field at the end of three rounds. But they had unexpected company in a twenty-year-old Brookline native named Francis Ouimet, who had matched their fifty-four-hole score of 225. Ouimet went out in forty-three at the start of the final round and seemed to be falling back into the pack. But he played the back nine of the par seventy-four, 6,200-yard course even, draining a testy five-footer on the eighteenth to finish in a three-way tie with Vardon and Ray.

The crowds were huge the following day, and some observers estimated the gallery at more than five thousand. Walking with his ten-year-old caddie, Eddie Lowery, Ouimet stayed even with his opponents through the first nine as all three players carded thirty-eights. But on the back side the youngster from Brookline began to pull away. He posted two birdies and seven pars for a stunning thirty-four and the win, the first ever by an amateur in a U.S. Open. By beating two of England's top players, Ouimet had also proved to many people that America could compete with the world's best, and as a result, he became the country's first golf hero.

It was fifty years before the USGA brought the Open back to Brookline. The club had added nine holes since the 1913 event, and parts of the newer course were incorporated with holes from the original eighteen to form a sort of composite track. Par was seventy-one, and it ran just under 6,900 yards.

Wind was the story at the 1963 championship, and galelike gusts sent scores soaring. Tommy Aaron shot ninety-one one round and Sam Snead eighty-three, while defending champion Jack Nicklaus missed the cut, going seventy-six and seventy-seven. No one was able to shoot par on the final day, and only three golfers made it around in seventy-two. One of those was Julius Boros, who came in birdie-birdie-par to secure a place in a play-off with Arnold Palmer and Jack Cupit. Boros, who was forty-three years old at the time, tamed the brutal Country Club course with a thirty-three on the front the next day and cruised home with a thirty-seven to finish one under par, three shots better than Cupit and six ahead of Palmer. One of the referees for the play-off was Francis Ouimet, who had been honored during the week with a

NUMBER SEVEN AT THE COUNTRY CLUB IS A 201-YARD PAR THREE. LIKE MOST OF THE HOLES AT BROOKLINE, THE FAIRWAY IS HUGGED CLOSELY BY TREES AND THE GREEN IS GUARDED BY HAZARDS, MAKING STRAIGHT AND ACCURATE APPROACH SHOTS ESSENTIAL. (ROBERT WALKER)

JULIUS BOROS'S PAR ON THE EIGHTEENTH IN 1963 PUT HIM INTO A PLAY-OFF WITH ARNOLD PALMER AND JACK CUPIT; HE SHOT A SEVENTY THE NEXT DAY FOR HIS SECOND OPEN WIN. (ROBERT WALKER)

dinner attended by several past Open champions and his former caddie, Eddie Lowery.

The USGA must have had something about anniversaries, because it sent the Open back to Brookline in 1988, seventy-five years after Ouimet's famous victory. Once again the tournament was decided by a play-off, and once again the winner was an American (Curtis Strange) holding off an Englishman (Nick Faldo). It was a different course than the one in '63, thanks to a meticulous restoration by Rees Jones. Using old photographs as his primary guide, he rebuilt several tees and greens, reshaped a number of bunkers, and narrowed some of the fairways, all with the hope of giving the club and its three nines— known as the Clyde, the Primrose, and the Squirrel—the feel and style of the old course. Once again, the USGA created a composite track, which measured just over seven thousand yards, and the reviews were rave, with some competitors calling it the best U.S. Open course they had ever played.

Brookline isn't yet scheduled to host another Open, but given the quality of the course and the history of the club, it will likely get a fourth championship before long. The prediction is that it will be the site of the 2013 Open, in celebration of Ouimet's extraordinary win a century before. What better way to honor a place so rich in golfing lore?

BROOKLINE'S THIRD HOLE, CALLED "THE POND" FOR THE WATER THAT LIES BEYOND THE GREEN, IS ONE OF THE MOST DIFFICULT ON THE COURSE. A 448-YARD PAR FOUR, IT IS FLANKED HEAVILY BY TREES AND RIDDLED WITH BUNKERS.
(ROBERT WALKER)

Winged Foot Golf Club

1929, 1959, 1974, 1984

The year was 1923 when a group of members from the New York Athletic Club bought 280 acres of rolling farmland in the Westchester County town of Mamaroneck and asked A.W. Tillinghast if he would build them a "man-sized" golf course. The Philadelphia designer, who was gaining fame for his work on layouts such as Baltusrol and Quaker Ridge, agreed, and to show his new clients that he meant business, he carved not one but two courses from that wonderful property. -

Man-sized indeed. They both bore the trademarks of their creator—long carries, huge bunkers, sloped greens—and years later Tillinghast said they represented his finest work.

Those tracks became the centerpiece of the new Winged Foot Golf Club, and just six years after opening it hosted the 1929 U.S. Open on the par seventy-two, 6,786-yard West Course. As was the case most anytime he competed that decade, Bobby Jones was the pretournament favorite. True to form, he played well, leading the tournament after the first and third rounds. But he stumbled badly during the final eighteen, making two triple bogeys along the way and losing a six-stroke lead. When he walked onto the eighteenth green Saturday afternoon he was tied with Al Espinosa, who was already in the clubhouse with a seventy-two-hole score of 294. Jones needed to make a twelve-foot putt for par to salvage a tie. It was a tricky shot with at least a foot of break to it, but he calmy stood over the ball and curled it in. He and Espinosa met in a thirty-six-hole play-off the following day, and it was no contest. Jones shot seventy-two and sixty-nine as Espinosa fell completely

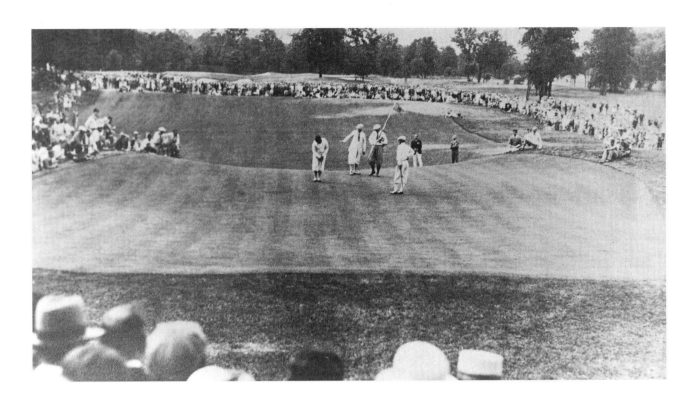

apart, posting eighty-four and eighty, and finishing a remarkable twenty-three shots behind.

The championship returned to Winged Foot in 1959, and again putting was the story. But this time it wasn't one big putt but rather several good ones that gave Billy Casper his first Open title. The beefy Californian started off with a seventy-one and followed that with sixty-eight and sixty-nine to lead by three shots after fifty-four holes. He increased his advantage to six strokes after six holes on Saturday afternoon, but then his game cooled off, and he ended with a seventy-four. His seventy-two-hole total came to 282, and although he wasn't pleased with his game that final round, he was happy about his play on the greens throughout the tournament; Casper had hit only 114 putts all week and had one-putted thirty-one times while three-putting only once.

But even though he had the lead, he couldn't yet celebrate because there were other golfers on the course. No one had a real shot at Casper, although Bob Rosburg came close. He needed to sink a thirty-foot putt on eighteen to force a play-off, but he left his ball short, and Casper, who had been watching the action from a clubhouse balcony, had his win.

The 1974 U.S. Open was dubbed the *Massacre at Winged Foot* by author Dick Schapp, and with good reason. The greens were as hard and slick as marble, and no one broke par, which had been lowered to seventy, during the first round of play. Consider, for example, that Jack

JONES FORCED A PLAY-OFF IN THE 1929 OPEN WITH THIS PUTT. HIS COMPETITOR, AL ESPINOSA, BROKE UNDER THE PRESSURE OF THE THIRTY-SIX-HOLE TIEBREAKER, LOSING TO JONES BY AN ASTONISHING TWENTY-THREE STROKES. (WINGED FOOT GOLF CLUB)

Number ten on Winged Foot's West Course, dubbed the Pulpit, is one of the most famous in golf. Fortified by bunkers and sloping dramatically to the front, the green often forces three-putts. A.W. Tillinghast called it the finest par three he ever designed.
(Winged Foot Golf Club)

Nicklaus hit a twenty-foot birdie putt from behind the pin on the first hole and then watched it roll clear off the green. He ended up with a seventy-five, which was three strokes below the average score that day. Many of the numbers were so high that someone went up to Sandy Tatum, chairman of the United States Golf Association Championship Committee, and asked him if the USGA was trying to embarrass the best players in the world. "No," Tatum replied. "We are trying to identify them."

After two rounds it seemed the USGA had done just that. The thirty-six-hole lead was shared by Hale Irwin, Arnold Palmer, Gary Player, and Ray Floyd, heavyweights all at 143, with Tom Watson and Tom Kite each a shot back. Watson fired a sixty-nine on Saturday and led Irwin by a stroke going into Sunday's final round. But the pressure of a U.S. Open lead got to the twenty-five-year-old, and he soared to seventy-nine. Palmer, Player, and Kite all fell back as well, but Irwin kept making pars, which was all he had to do on such a tough layout. He finished in grand style, drilling a two iron to within twenty feet on eighteen and then two-putting for his victory. His final score was a

seven-over 287; in the years since World War II, only Julius Boros's nine-over total at The Country Club in 1963 had been higher.

The course did not play as tough for the 1984 Open. Hale Irwin led again after thirty-six holes, but his score was seven strokes lower than it had been in '74. He was on top after fifty-four holes as well but could muster only a seventy-nine on the final day and fell out of contention. The battle was between Fuzzy Zoeller and Greg Norman, who were tied after seventeen. Norman was playing in the group ahead of Zoeller, and after hitting a magnificent drive on eighteen pushed his second shot into the grandstand. He took a drop and then chipped onto the green. With Fuzzy watching from the middle of the fairway, Norman proceeded to snake in a forty-five-foot putt for par. The Shark ran excitedly around the green, and Zoeller pulled a white towel from his bag and began waving it in mock surrender. He then parred the hole himself, and the two met in a play-off the next day. Once again, a putt on eighteen sent the Open into overtime.

It wasn't as bad as the play-off between Bobby Jones and Al Espinosa, but it still was a rout. Zoeller took a five-stroke lead after nine

THE MAGNIFICENT CLUBHOUSE AT WINGED FOOT HAS PRESIDED OVER TEN MAJOR COMPETITIONS SINCE 1929, INCLUDING FOUR U.S. OPENS.

(DAN McKEAN)

TWICE, PUTTS ON WINGED FOOT'S
EIGHTEENTH GREEN (SEEN HERE FROM
ABOVE) HAVE SENT U.S. OPENS INTO
PLAY-OFFS. MOST RECENTLY, FUZZY
ZOELLER CLINCHED A PLAY-OFF AGAINST
GREG NORMAN IN THE 1984 OPEN WITH
A SIXTY-SEVEN—THE LOWEST SCORE IN
U.S. OPEN PLAY-OFF HISTORY. (WINGED FOOT
GOLF CLUB)

holes and increased it to eight after fifteen. Walking up the eighteenth fairway together, it was Norman's turn to wave a white towel. Zoeller finished with a sixty-seven, and it still stands as the lowest score in Open play-off history.

In addition to hosting four U.S. Opens, the West Course at Winged Foot has also been the site of the 1940 U.S. Amateur and the 1949 Walker Cup and will host the PGA Championship in 1997. The East Course is no slouch, however, and in addition to holding two Women's Opens, also had the 1980 Senior Open, which was won by Roberto Di Vicenzo.

That makes ten major competitions since its founding in 1923. Clearly, Tillinghast wasn't the only one who thought that Winged Foot was his best work.

Worcester Country Club

1925

Designed by Donald Ross in 1914, the Worcester Country Club hosted its first and only U.S. Open eleven years later. Not surprisingly, the betting favorite was Bobby Jones, who seemed to be winning every tournament in sight. But he struggled that first day on Worcester's 6,430-yard, par seventy-one track, carding a seventy-seven and falling into a tie with six others for thirty-sixth place. He might have finished a bit higher that day had he not called a one-stroke penalty on himself when his ball moved in the rough after he had grazed the grass with his club. But that's just the way Jones was.

He played better the second day, posting a seventy and climbing into a tie for tenth. The leaders were Willie MacFarlane and Leo Diegel, six strokes ahead with 141s. Both men had hit the ball brilliantly that day, with MacFarlane shooting an Open record sixty-seven and Diegel a sixty-eight. But Worcester would not play so easily for them the following morning: MacFarlane carded a seventy-two, while Diegel soared

THE DONALD ROSS-DESIGNED COURSE NESTLED OUTSIDE WORCESTER, MASSACHUSETTS, HAS CHANGED LITTLE SINCE IT HOSTED THE 1925 U.S. OPEN.
(WORCESTER COUNTRY CLUB)

Golf Courses of the U.S. Open

SCOTSMAN WILLIE MACFARLANE
FINALLY TOPPLED TOURNAMENT
FAVORITE BOBBY JONES AT THE 1925
OPEN AFTER TWO EIGHTEEN-HOLE
PLAY-OFFS. (USGA)

to seventy-seven. Still, the bespectacled Scotsman remained on top, leading Johnny Farrell by a shot, Francis Ouimet by two, and Bobby Jones and Al Espinosa by three as he readied himself for the afternoon round.

The 1925 championship turned out to be one of those that nobody seemed to want to win. MacFarlane fell apart and could manage only a seventy-eight. But that's exactly what Farrell shot, and Ouimet's seventy-six was not much better. Jones posted a seventy-four, enough to tie him with MacFarlane at 291. The two met in a play-off the following morning, and MacFarlane had a chance to win it all when he stood over a six-foot putt on eighteen. But he missed, and the players remained tied, both having posted seventy-fives. So they went back at it that afternoon. Jones shot thirty-five on the front to MacFarlane's thirty-nine to lead by four shots at the turn. MacFarlane got a second wind and, after birdies at ten and thirteen, pulled to within one. He got even when Jones bogeyed fifteen and then finished him off on eighteen with a par.

MacFarlane was the first Scotsman to win a U.S. Open since 1910, and he pulled it off without having had much practice. Prior to qualifying for the championship, he hadn't hit a ball in eight months, and he had played for just a week before the Open to get ready for the competition.

Worcester is a quiet club in central Massachusetts, and it has never hosted another major men's event. It was the site, however, of the 1960 Women's Open, which was won by Betsy Rawls.

Appendices

Atlanta Athletic Club
1976

TOP TEN FINISHERS

1. Jerry Pate
T–2. Al Geiberger
T–2. Tom Weiskopf
T–4. Butch Baird
T–4. John Mahaffey
6. Hubert Green
7. Tom Watson
T–8. Ben Crenshaw
T–8. Lyn Lott
10. Johnny Miller

LOW SCORERS

First Round: Mike Reid
Second Round: John Mahaffey & Ben Crenshaw
Third Round: Tom Weiskopf & Tom Watson
Fourth Round: Butch Baird

Baltusrol Golf Club
1903

TOP TEN FINISHERS

1. Willie Anderson
2. David Brown
3. Stewart Gardner
4. Alex Smith
5. Donald Ross
6. Jack Campbell
7. Laurie Auchterlonie
8. Findlay Douglas
T–9. Jack Hobens
T–9. Alex Ross
T–9. Willie Smith

LOW SCORERS

First Round: Willie Anderson
Second Round: F.O. Reinhart & William Braid
Third Round: David Brown
Fourth Round: David Brown

1915

TOP TEN FINISHERS

1. Jerome Travers
2. Tom McNamara
3. Bob MacDonald
T–4. James Barnes
T–4. Louis Tellier
6. Mike Brady
7. George Low
T–8. Jock Hutchison
T–8. Fred McLeod
T–10. Alex Campbell
T–10. Emmett French
T–10. Walter Hagen
T–10. Tom Kerrigan
T–10. Gilbert Nicholls
T–10. Jack Park
T–10. Wilfred Reid
T–10. George Sargent

LOW SCORERS

First Round: James Barnes & Charles Evans, Jr.

Second Round: Louis Tellier, Mike Brady & Tom McNamara
Third Round: Jerome Travers, Bob MacDonald & Gilbert Nicholls
Fourth Round: James Donaldson

1936

TOP TEN FINISHERS

1. Tony Manero
2. Harry Cooper
3. Clarence Clark
4. Macdonald Smith
T–5. Wiffy Cox
T–5. Ky Laffoon
T–5. Henry Picard
T–8. Ralph Guldahl
T–8. Paul Runyan
10. Denny Shute

LOW SCORERS

First Round: Clarence Clark, Paul Runyan & Ray Mangrum
Second Round: Tony Manero & Denny Shute
Third Round: Wiffy Cox & Herman Barron
Fourth Round: Tony Manero

1954

TOP TEN FINISHERS

1. Ed Furgol
2. Gene Littler
T–3. Lloyd Mangrum
T–3. Dick Mayer
5. Bobby Locke
T–6. Tommy Bolt
T–6. Fred Haas
T–6. Ben Hogan
T–6. Shelley Mayfield
T–6. Billy Joe Patton

LOW SCORERS

First Round: Billy Joe Patton
Second Round: Dick Chapman
Third Round: Leland Gibson & Johnny Weitzel
Fourth Round: Shelley Mayfield

1967

TOP TEN FINISHERS

1. Jack Nicklaus
2. Arnold Palmer
3. Don January
4. Billy Casper
5. Lee Trevino
T–6. Deane Beman
T–6. Gardner Dickinson
T–6. Bob Goalby
T–9. Dave Marr
T–9. Kel Nagle
T–9. Art Wall

LOW SCORERS

First Round: Marty Fleckman
Second Round: Jack Nicklaus & Dick Lotz
Third Round: Gardner Dickinson
Fourth Round: Jack Nicklaus

1980

TOP TEN FINISHERS

1. Jack Nicklaus
2. Isao Aoki
T–3. Keith Fergus
T–3. Lon Hinkle
T–3. Tom Watson
T–6. Mark Hayes
T–6. Mike Reid
T–8. Hale Irwin
T–8. Mike Morley
T–8. Andy North
T–8. Ed Sneed

LOW SCORERS

First Round: Jack Nicklaus & Tom Weiskopf
Second Round: Mike Reid & Craig Stadler
Third Round: Hubert Green
Fourth Round: Andy North

1993

TOP TEN FINISHERS

1. Lee Janzen
2. Payne Stewart
T–3. Paul Azinger
T–3. Craig Parry
T–5. Scott Hoch
T–5. Tom Watson
T–7. Ernie Els
T–7. Ray Floyd
T–7. Fred Funk
T–7. Nolan Henke

LOW SCORERS

First Round: Craig Parry, Scott Hoch & Joey Sindelar
Second Round: Payne Stewart, Tom Watson, Nick Price & John Cook
Third Round: David Edwards
Fourth Round: Steve Lowery

Bellerive Country Club
1965

TOP TEN FINSIHERS

1. Gary Player
2. Kel Nagle
3. Frank Beard
T–4. Julius Boros
T–4. Al Geiberger
T–6. Bruce Devlin
T–6. Ray Floyd
T–8. Tony Lema
T–8. Gene Littler
T–8. Dudley Wysong

LOW SCORERS

First Round: Kel Nagle

Second Round: Frank Beard &
George Knudson

Third Round: Doug Sanders

Fourth Round: Ray Floyd

Brae Burn Country Club
1919

TOP TEN FINISHERS

1. Walter Hagen
2. Mike Brady
T–3. Jock Hutchison
T–3. Tom McNamara
T–5. George McLean
T–5. Louis Tellier
7. John Cowan
8. Fred McLeod
T–9. George Bowden
T–9. Charles Evans Jr.

LOW SCORERS

First Round: Charles Hoffner

Second Round: Walter Hagen &
Tom McNamara

Third Round: Mike Brady

Fourth Round: Tom McNamara,
Clarence Hackney & J. Sanderson

Country Club of Buffalo
1912

TOP TEN FINISHERS

1. John McDermott
2. Tom McNamara
T–3. Mike Brady
T–3. Alex Smith
5. Alex Campbell
6. George Sargent
T–7. Jack Dowling
T–7. Otto Hackbarth
9. C.R. Murray

T–10. Tom Anderson, Jr.
T–10. Frank Peebles
T–10. Walter Travis

LOW SCORERS

First Round: Mike Brady & George
Sargent

Second Round: Alex Smith

Third Round: Mike Brady, Tom
McNamara, Willie MacFarlane &
David Ogilvie

Fourth Round: Tom McNamara

Canterbury Golf Club
1940

TOP TEN FINISHERS

1. Lawson Little
2. Gene Sarazen
3. Horton Smith
4. Craig Wood
T–5. Ralph Guldahl
T–5. Ben Hogan
T–5. Lloyd Mangrum
T–5. Byron Nelson
9. Dick Metz
T–10. Ed Dudley
T–10. Frank Walsh

LOW SCORERS

First Round: Sam Snead

Second Round: Lawson Little &
Frank Walsh

Third Round: Gene Sarazen, Byron
Nelson, Harold McSpaden & Edward
Oliver

Fourth Round: Horton Smith

1946

TOP TEN FINISHERS

1. Lloyd Mangrum
T–2. Vic Ghezzi
T–2. Byron Nelson

T–4. Herman Barron
T–4. Ben Hogan
T–6. Jimmy Demaret
T–6. Edward Oliver Jr.
T–8. Chick Harbert
T–8. Dick Metz
T–10. Dutch Harrison
T–10. Lawson Little

LOW SCORERS

First Round: Toney Penna &
Sam Snead

Second Round: Ben Hogan

Third Round: Chick Harbert &
Chandler Harper

Fourth Round: Jimmy Demaret

Champions Golf Club
1969

TOP TEN FINISHERS

1. Orville Moody
T–2. Deane Beman
T–2. Al Geiberger
T–2. Bob Rosburg
5. Bob Murphy
T–6. Miller Barber
T–6. Bruce Crampton
T–6. Arnold Palmer
9. Bunky Henry
T–10. George Archer
T–10. Bruce Devlin
T–10. Dave Marr

LOW SCORERS

First Round: Bob Murphy

Second Round: Jack Nicklaus &
Bob E. Smith

Third Round: Bobby Mitchell

Fourth Round: Bruce Devlin &
Al Geiberger

Cherry Hills Country Club
1938

TOP TEN FINISHERS

1. Ralph Guldahl
2. Dick Metz
T–3. Harry Cooper
T–3. Toney Penna
T–5. Byron Nelson
T–5. Emery Zimmerman
T–7. Frank Moore
T–7. Henry Picard
T–7. Paul Runyan
10. Gene Sarazen

LOW SCORERS

First Round: Henry Picard & Jimmy Hines

Second Round: Harold McSpaden

Third Round: Jimmy Hines

Fourth Round: Toney Penna

1960

TOP TEN FINISHERS

1. Arnold Palmer
2. Jack Nicklaus
T–3. Julius Boros
T–3. Dow Finsterwald
T–3. Jack Fleck
T–3. Dutch Harrison
T–3. Ted Kroll
T–3. Mike Souchak
T–9. Jerry Barber
T–9. Don Cherry
T–9. Ben Hogan

LOW SCORERS

First Round: Mike Souchak

Second Round: Mike Souchak, Ben Hogan & Rex Baxter

Third Round: Julius Boros

Fourth Round: Arnold Palmer

1978

TOP TEN FINISHERS

1. Andy North
T–2. J.C. Snead
T–2. Dave Stockton
T–4. Hale Irwin
T–4. Tom Weiskopf
T–6. Andy Bean
T–6. Bill Kratzert
T–6. Johnny Miller
T–6. Jack Nicklaus
T–6. Gary Player
T–6. Tom Watson

LOW SCORERS

First Round: Hale Irwin

Second Round: Jack Nicklaus, Johnny Miller, Seve Ballesteros & Bill Rogers

Third Round: Johnny Miller

Fourth Round: Tom Weiskopf & Mike McCullough

Chicago Golf Club
1897

TOP TEN FINISHERS

1. Joe Lloyd
2. Willie Anderson
T–3. Willie Dunn
T–3. James Foulis
5. W.T. Hoare
T–6. Bernard Nicholls
T–6. Alfred Ricketts
T–6. David Foulis
T–8. Horace Rawlins
T–8. H.J. Whigham

LOW SCORERS

First Round: Willie Anderson

Second Round: Joe Lloyd

1900

TOP TEN FINISHERS

1. Harry Vardon
2. J.H. Taylor
3. David Bell
4. Laurie Auchterlonie
5. Willie Smith
6. George Low
7. Tom Hutchinson
8. Harry Turpie
9. Stewart Gardner
10. Val Fitzjohn

LOW SCORERS

First Round: J.H. Taylor

Second Round: Alex Campbell

Third Round: Harry Vardon

Fourth Round: J.H. Taylor & David Bell

1911

TOP TEN FINISHERS

1. John McDermott
2. Mike Brady
3. George Simpson
4 . Fred McLeod
T–5. Jock Hutchinson
T–5. Gilbert Nicholls
T–7. H.H. Barker
T–7. George Sargent
T–9. Peter Robertson
T–9. Alex Ross

LOW SCORERS

First Round: Alex Ross

Second Round: John McDermott & Fred McLeod

Third Round: Alex Campbell

Fourth Round: George Sargent & James Donaldson

Colonial Country Club
1941

TOP TEN FINISHERS

1. Craig Wood
2. Denny Shute
T–3. Johnny Bulla
T–3. Ben Hogan
T–5. Herman Barron
T–5. Paul Runyan
T–7. Dutch Harrison
T–7. Harold McSpaden
T–7. Gene Sarazen
T–10. Ed Dudley
T–10. Lloyd Mangrum
T–10. Dick Metz

LOW SCORERS

First Round: Denny Shute
Second Round: Sam Snead
Third Round: Ben Hogan
Fourth Round: Craig Wood &
Ben Hogan

Columbia Country Club
1921

TOP TEN FINISHERS

1. James Barnes
T–2. Walter Hagen
T–2. Fred McLeod
4. Charles Evans Jr.
T–5. Emmett French
T–5. Bobby Jones
T–5. Alex Smith
T–8. George Duncan
T–8. Clarence Hackney
10. Emil Loeffler Jr.

LOW SCORERS

First Round: James Barnes
Second Round: Bobby Jones
Third Round: Walter Hagen
Fourth Round: Alfred Hackbarth

Congressional Country Club
1964

TOP TEN FINISHERS

1. Ken Venturi
2. Tommy Jacobs
3. Bob Charles
4. Billy Casper
T–5. Gay Brewer
T–5. Arnold Palmer
7. Bill Collins
8. Dow Finsterwald
T–9. Johnny Pott
T–9. Bob Rosburg

LOW SCORERS

First Round: Arnold Palmer
Second Round: Tommy Jacobs
Third Round: Ken Venturi
Fourth Round: Bob Charles &
Gay Brewer

Englewood Golf Club
1909

TOP TEN FINISHERS

1. George Sargent
2. Tom McNamara
3. Alex Smith
T–4. Willie Anderson
T–4. Jack Hobens
T–4. Isaac Mackie
T–7. Tom Anderson Jr.
T–7. H.H. Barker
T–7. Andrew Campbell
T–7. Tom Peebles
T–7. Walter Travis

LOW SCORERS

First Round: David Hunter
Second Round: Tom McNamara
Third Round: George Sargent
Fourth Round: Willie Anderson

Fresh Meadow Country Club
1932

TOP TEN FINISHERS

1. Gene Sarazen
T–2. Bobby Cruickshank
T–2. Philip Perkins
4. Leo Diegel
5. Wiffy Cox
6. Jose Jurado
T–7. Billy Burke
T–7. Harry Cooper
T–7. Olin Dutra
10. Walter Hagen

LOW SCORERS

First Round: Olin Dutra
Second Round: Philip Perkins
Third Round: Bobby Cruickshank,
Paul Runyan & Fred Morrison
Fourth Round: Gene Sarazen

Garden City Golf Club
1902

TOP TEN FINISHERS

1. Laurie Auchterlonie
T–2. Stewart Gardner
T–2. Walter Travis
4. Willie Smith
T–5. Willie Anderson
T–5. John Shippen
7. Charles Thorn
8. Harry Turpie
9. Donald Ross
10. Alex Ross

LOW SCORERS

First Round: Jack Campbell
Second Round: Stewart Gardner
Third Round: Gilbert Nicholls
Fourth Round: Walter Travis

Glen View Club
1904

TOP TEN FINISHERS

1. Willie Anderson
2. Gilbert Nicholls
3. Fred MacKenzie
T–4. Laurie Auchterlonie
T–4. Bernard Nicholls
T–6. Percy Barrett
T–6. Stewart Gardner
T–6. Robert Simpson
9. James Foulis
10. Donald Ross

LOW SCORERS

First Round: Willie Anderson & Stewart Gardner
Second Round: James Foulis
Third Round: Fred MacKenzie
Fourth Round: Willie Anderson & Alex Campbell

Hazeltine National Golf Club
1970

TOP TEN FINISHERS

1. Tony Jacklin
2. Dave Hill
T–3. Bob Charles
T–3. Bob Lunn
5. Ken Still
6. Miller Barber
7. Gay Brewer
T–8. Billy Casper
T–8. Bruce Devlin
T–8. Lee Trevino
T–8. Larry Ziegler

LOW SCORERS

First Round: Tony Jacklin
Second Round: Randy Wolff
Third Round: Tony Jacklin, Bob Lunn, Julius Boros & Ray Floyd
Fourth Round: Bob Charles

1991

TOP TEN FINISHERS

1. Payne Stewart
2. Scott Simpson
T–3. Fred Couples
T–3. Larry Nelson
5. Fuzzy Zoeller
6. Scott Hoch
7. Nolan Henke
T–8. Ray Floyd
T–8. Jose Maria Olazabal
T–8. Corey Pavin

LOW SCORERS

First Round: Payne Stewart & Nolan Henke
Second Round: Corey Pavin
Third Round: Hale Irwin
Fourth Round: Fuzzy Zoeller

Interlachen Country Club
1930

TOP TEN FINISHERS

1. Bobby Jones
2. Macdonald Smith
3. Horton Smith
4. Harry Cooper
5. Johnny Golden
6. Tommy Armour
7. Charles Lacey
8. Johnny Farrell
T–9. William Mehlhorn
T–9. Craig Wood

LOW SCORERS

First Round: Macdonald Smith & Tommy Armour
Second Round: Charles Lacey & Horton Smith
Third Round: Bobby Jones
Fourth Round: Macdonald Smith

Inverness Club
1920

TOP TEN FINISHERS

1. Edward Ray
T–2. Jack Burke Sr.
T–2. Leo Diegel
T–2. Jock Hutchison
T–2. Harry Vardon
T–6. James Barnes
T–6. Charles Evans Jr.
T–8. Bobby Jones
T–8. Willie MacFarlane
10. Bob MacDonald

LOW SCORERS

First Round: Jock Hutchison
Second Round: James Barnes
Third Round: Bobby Jones
Fourth Round: Jack Burke Sr.

1931

TOP TEN FINISHERS

1. Billy Burke
2. George Von Elm
3. Leo Diegel
T–4. Wiffy Cox
T–4. William Mehlhorn
T–4. Gene Sarazen
T–7. Mortie Dutra
T–7. Walter Hagen
T–7. Philip Perkins
T–10. Al Espinosa
T–10. Johnny Farrell
T–10. Macdonald Smith

LOW SCORERS

First Round: Mortie Dutra, Herman Barron, Charles Guest & Eddie Williams
Second Round: George Von Elm
Third Round: Willie Klein
Fourth Round: Philip Perkins & Gene Sarazen

1957

TOP TEN FINISHERS

1. Dick Mayer
2. Cary Middlecoff
3. Jimmy Demaret
T–4. Julius Boros
T–4. Walter Burkemo
T–6. Fred Hawkins
T–6. Ken Venturi
T–8. Roberto DeVincenzo
T–8. Chick Harbert
T–8. Billy Maxwell
T–8. Billy Joe Patton
T–8. Sam Snead

LOW SCORERS

First Round: Jimmy Demaret & Chick Harbert
Second Round: Dick Mayer & Billy Joe Patton
Third Round: Cary Middlecoff
Fourth Round: Walter Burkemo

1979

TOP TEN FINISHERS

1. Hale Irwin
T–2. Jerry Pate
T–2. Gary Player
T–4. Larry Nelson
T–4. Bill Rogers
T–4. Tom Weiskopf
7. David Graham
8. Tom Purtzer
T–9. Keith Fergus
T–9. Jack Nicklaus

LOW SCORERS

First Round: Tom Purtzer, Keith Fergus, Lou Graham & Andy Bean
Second Round: Hale Irwin & Larry Nelson
Third Round: Hale Irwin & Tom Weiskopf

Fourth Round: Gary Player, Jack Nicklaus & Jim Simons

Inwood Country Club
1923

TOP TEN FINISHERS

1. Bobby Jones
2. Bobby Cruickshank
3. Jock Hutchison
4. Jack Forrester
T–5. Johnny Farrell
T–5. Francis Gallett
T–5. W.M. Reekie
T–8. Leo Diegel
T–8. William Mehlhorn
T–8. Al Watrous

LOW SCORERS

First Round: Jock Hutchison
Second Round: Jock Hutchison, Bobby Cruickshank & Francis Gallett
Third Round: Charles Mothersole
Fourth Round: Bobby Cruickshank

Medinah Country Club
1949

TOP TEN FINISHERS

1. Cary Middlecoff
T–2. Clayton Heafner
T–2. Sam Snead
T–4. Bobby Locke
T–4. Jim Turnesa
T–6. Dave Douglas
T–6. Buck White
T–8. Pete Cooper
T–8. Claude Harmon
T–8. Johnny Palmer

LOW SCORERS

First Round: Les Kennedy
Second Round: Cary Middlecoff
Third Round: Cary Middlecoff
Fourth Round: Sam Snead

1975

TOP TEN FINISHERS

1. Lou Graham
2. John Mahaffey
T–3. Frank Beard
T–3. Ben Crenshaw
T–3. Hale Irwin
T–3. Bob Murphy
T–7. Jack Nicklaus
T–7. Peter Oosterhuis
T–9. Pat Fitzsimons
T–9. Arnold Palmer
T–9. Tom Watson

LOW SCORERS

First Round: Tom Watson & Pat Fitzsimons
Second Round: Jerry Heard
Third Round: Frank Beard
Fourth Round: Bob Murphy & Tommy Aaron

1990

TOP TEN FINISHERS

1. Hale Irwin
2. Mike Donald
T–3. Billy Ray Brown
T–3. Nick Faldo
T–5. Mark Brooks
T–5. Greg Norman
T–5. Tim Simpson
T–8. Scott Hoch
T–8. Steve Jones
T–8. Jose Maria Olazabal
T–8. Tom Sieckmann
T–8. Craig Stadler
T–8. Fuzzy Zoeller

LOW SCORERS

First Round: Tim Simpson, Jeff Sluman & Scott Simpson
Second Round: Mike Hulbert

Third Round: Nick Faldo, Fuzzy Zoeller, Tom Sieckmann, Curtis Strange, Mike Reid, Jack Nicklaus & Craig Parry
Fourth Round: Hale Irwin & Steve Jones

Merion Golf Club
1934
Top Ten Finishers
1. Olin Dutra
2. Gene Sarazen
T–3. Harry Cooper
T–3. Wiffy Cox
T–3. Bobby Cruickshank
T–6. Billy Burke
T–6. Macdonald Smith
T–8. Tom Creavy
T–8. Ralph Guldahl
T–8. Jimmy Hines
T–8. Johnny Revolta

Low Scorers
First Round: Wiffy Cox, Bobby Cruickshank & Charles Lacey
Second Round: Jimmy Hines
Third Round: Ralph Guldahl
Fourth Round: Tom Creavy

1950
Top Ten Finishers
1. Ben Hogan
2. Lloyd Mangrum
3. George Fazio
4. Dutch Harrison
T–5. Jim Ferrier
T–5. Joe Kirkwood Jr.
T–5. Henry Ransom
8. Bill Nary
9. Julius Boros
T–10. Cary Middlecoff
T–10. Johnny Palmer

Low Scorers
First Round: Lee Mackey Jr.
Second Round: Johnny Bulla
Third Round: Lloyd Mangrum
Fourth Round: George Fazio & Joe Kirkwood Jr.

1971
Top Ten Finishers
1. Lee Trevino
2. Jack Nicklaus
T–3. Jim Colbert
T–3. Bob Rosburg
T–5. George Archer
T–5. Johnny Miller
T–5. Jim Simons
8. Ray Floyd
T–9. Gay Brewer
T–9. Larry Hinson
T–9. Bobby Nichols
T–9. Bert Yancey

Low Scorers
First Round: Labron Harris Jr.
Second Round: Jerry McGee & Bob Erickson
Third Round: Jim Simons
Fourth Round: Lanny Wadkins

1981
Top Ten Finishers
1. David Graham
T–2. George Burns
T–2. Bill Rogers
T–4. John Cook
T–4. John Schroeder
T–6. Frank Conner
T–6. Lon Hinkle
T–6. Jack Nicklaus
T–6. Sammy Rachels
T–6. Chi Chi Rodriguez

Low Scorers
First Round: Jim Thorpe
Second Round: George Burns
Third Round: Ben Crenshaw
Fourth Round: David Graham & Isao Aoki

Midlothian Country Club
1914
Top Ten Finishers
1. Walter Hagen
2. Charles Evans Jr.
T–3. Fred McLeod
T–3. George Sargent
T–5. Mike Brady
T–5. James Donaldson
T–5. Francis Ouimet
8. Louis Tellier
T–9. John McDermott
T–9. Arthur Smith

Low Scorers
First Round: Walter Hagen
Second Round: Joe Mitchell
Third Round: Charles Evans Jr.
Fourth Round: Charles Evans Jr.

Minikahda Club
1916
Top Ten Finishers
1. Charles Evans Jr.
2. Jock Hutchinson
3. James Barnes
T–4. Gilbert Nicholls
T–4. Wilfred Reid
T–4. George Sargent
7. Walter Hagen
8. Bob MacDonald
T–9. Mike Brady
T–9. J.J. O'Brien
T–9. Tom Vardon

LOW SCORERS

First Round: Charles Evans Jr. & Wilfred Reid

Second Round: Charles Evans Jr.

Third Round: Otto Hackbarth

Fourth Round: Jock Hutchinson

Myopia Hunt Club
1898

TOP TEN FINISHERS

1. Fred Herd
2. Alex Smith
3. Willie Anderson
4. Joe Lloyd
5. Willie Smith
6. W.B. Hoare
7. Willie Dunn
T–8. J. Jones
T–8. H.C. Leeds
T–8. R.G. McAndrews
T–8. Bernard Nicholls

LOW SCORERS

First Round: Alex Smith

Second Round: Joe Lloyd

Third Round: Fred Herd

Fourth Round: Willie Smith

1901

TOP TEN FINISHERS

1. Willie Anderson
2. Alex Smith
3. Willie Smith
4. Stewart Gardner
T–5. Laurie Auchterlonie
T–5. Bernard Nicholls
7. David Brown
8. Alex Campbell
T–9. George Low
T–9. Jack Park

LOW SCORERS

First Round: Laurie Auchterlonie

Second Round: Alex Smith & Stewart Gardner

Third Round: Stewart Gardner

Fourth Round: Alex Smith & John Jones

1905

TOP TEN FINISHERS

1. Willie Anderson
2. Alex Smith
T–3. Percy Barrett
T–3. Peter Robertson
5. Stewart Gardner
6. Alex Campbell
T–7. Gilbert Nicholls
T–7. Jack Hobens
9. George Cummings
10. Arthur Smith

LOW SCORERS

First Round: Joe Lloyd

Second Round: Alex Campbell & Gilbert Nicholls

Third Round: George Cummings

Fourth Round: Willie Anderson, Peter Robertson, W.H. Way & Stewart Gardner

1908

TOP TEN FINISHERS

1. Fred McLeod
2. Willie Smith
3. Alex Smith
4. Willie Anderson
5. John Jones
T–6. Jack Hobens
T–6. Peter Robertson
T–8. Percy Barrett
T–8. Jock Hutchison
T–10. Richard Kimball
T–10. Tom McNamara

LOW SCORERS

First Round: Willie Smith

Second Round: Gilbert Nicholls

Third Round: Peter Robertson

Fourth Round: Fred McLeod

Newport Golf Club
1895

TOP TEN FINISHERS

1. Horace Rawlins
2. Willie Dunn
T–3. James Foulis
T–3. A.W. Smith
5. W.F. Davis
6. Willie Campbell
T–7. John Harland
T–7. John Patrick
9. Samuel Tucker
10. John Reid

LOW SCORERS

First Round: Willie Campbell, Willie Dunn & James Foulis

Second Round: Horace Rawlins

North Shore Country Club
1933

TOP TEN FINISHERS

1. Johnny Goodman
2. Ralph Guldhal
3. Craig Wood
T–4. Tommy Armour
T–4. Walter Hagen
6. Mortie Dutra
T–7. Olin Dutra
T–7. Gus Moreland
T–9. Clarence Clark
T–9. Johnny Farrell
T–9. Willie Goggin
T–9. Joe Kirkwood

LOW SCORERS

First Round: Tommy Armour

Second Round: Johnny Goodman

Third Round: Johnny Goodman & Ralph Guldahl

Fourth Round: Walter Hagen

Northwood Club
1952

TOP TEN FINISHERS

1. Julius Boros
2. Edward Oliver Jr.
3. Ben Hogan
4. Johnny Bulla
5. George Fazio
6. Dick Metz
T–7. Tommy Bolt
T–7. Ted Kroll
T–7. Lew Worsham
T–10. Lloyd Mangrum
T–10. Sam Snead
T–10. Earl Stewart Jr.

LOW SCORERS

First Round: Al Brosch

Second Round: Johnny Bulla

Third Round: Julius Boros

Fourth Round: Ted Kroll & Bill Trombley

Oak Hill Country Club
1956

TOP TEN FINISHERS

1. Cary Middlecoff
T–2. Julius Boros
T–2. Ben Hogan
T–4. Ed Furgol
T–4. Ted Kroll
T–4. Peter Thompson
7. Arnold Palmer
8. Ken Venturi
T–9. Jerry Barber
T–9. Wes Ellis
T–9. Doug Ford

LOW SCORERS

First Round: Bob Rosburg

Second Round: Ben Hogan

Third Round: Ken Venturi

Fourth Round: Julius Boros & Bill Ogden

1968

TOP TEN FINISHERS

1. Lee Trevino
2. Jack Nicklaus
3. Bert Yancey
4. Bobby Nichols
T–5. Don Bies
T–5. Steve Spray
T–7. Bob Charles
T–7. Jerry Pittman
T–9. Gay Brewer
T–9. Billy Casper
T–9. Bruce Devlin
T–9. Al Geiberger
T–9. Sam Snead
T–9. Dave Stockton

LOW SCORERS

First Round: Bert Yancey

Second Round: Jerry Pittman

Third Round: Bobby Nichols & Al Geiberger

Fourth Round: Steve Spray

1989

TOP TEN FINISHERS

1. Curtis Strange
T–2. Chip Beck
T–2. Mark McCumber
T–2. Ian Woosnam
5. Brian Claar
T–6. Jumbo Ozaki
T–6. Scott Simpson
8. Peter Jacobsen
T–9. Paul Azinger
T–9. Hubert Green

T–9. Tom Kite
T–9. Jose Maria Olazabal

LOW SCORERS

First Round: Payne Stewart, Jay Don Blake & Berhard Langer

Second Round: Curtis Strange

Third Round: Fred Couples

Fourth Round: Chip Beck, Ian Woosnam, Hubert Green & Steve Elkington

Oakland Hills
1924

TOP TEN FINISHERS

1. Cyril Walker
2. Bobby Jones
3. William Melhorn
T–4. Bobby Cruickshank
T–4. Walter Hagen
T–4. Macdonald Smith
T–7. Abe Espinosa
T–7. Peter O'Hara
9. Mike Brady
T–10. Charles Evans Jr.
T–10. Eddie Loos
T–10. Dave Robertson

LOW SCORERS

First Round: William Mehlhorn

Second Round: Abe Espinosa

Third Round: Cyril Walker, Peter O'Hara & Jock Hutchison

Fourth Round: Tom Kerrigan

1937

TOP TEN FINISHERS

1. Ralph Guldahl
2. Sam Snead
3. Bobby Cruickshank
4. Harry Cooper
5. Ed Dudley
6. Al Brosch
7. Clarence Clark
8. Johnny Goodman

9. Frank Strafaci

T–10. Charles Kocsis

T–10. Henry Picard

T–10. Gene Sarazen

T–10. Denny Shute

LOW SCORERS

First Round: Sam Snead & Denny Shute

Second Round: Jimmy Thompson

Third Round: Bobby Cruickshank

Fourth Round: Ralph Guldahl

1951

TOP TEN FINISHERS

1. Ben Hogan

2. Clayton Heafner

3. Bobby Locke

T–4. Julius Boros

T–4. Lloyd Mangrum

T–6. Al Besselink

T–6. Dave Douglas

T–6. Fred Hawkins

T–6. Paul Runyan

T–10. Al Brosch

T–10. Smiley Quick

T–10. Skee Riegel

T–10. Sam Snead

LOW SCORERS

First Round: Sam Snead

Second Round: Dave Douglas & Johnny Bulla

Third Round: Jimmy Demaret

Fourth Round: Ben Hogan

1961

TOP TEN FINISHERS

1. Gene Littler

T–2. Bob Goalby

T–2. Doug Sanders

T–4. Jack Nicklaus

T–4. Mike Souchak

T–6. Dow Finsterwald

T–6. Doug Ford

T–6. Eric Monti

T–9. Jacky Culpit

T–9. Gardner Dickinson

T–9. Gary Player

LOW SCORERS

First Round: Bruce Brue

Second Round: Doug Sanders, Eric Monti, Bob Rosburg & Bob Harris

Third Round: Jacky Culpit

Fourth Round: Gene Littler

1985

TOP TEN FINISHERS

1. Andy North

T–2. Dave Barr

T–2. T.C. Chen

T–2. Denis Watson

T–5. Seve Ballesteros

T–5. Payne Stewart

T–5. Lanny Wadkins

8. Johnny Miller

T–9. Rick Fehr

T–9. Corey Pavin

T–9. Jack Renner

T–9. Fuzzy Zoeller

LOW SCORERS

First Round: T.C. Chen

Second Round: Andy North & Denis Watson

Third Round: Johnny Miller & Scott Simpson

Fourth Round: Hal Sutton & David Graham

1996

TOP TEN FINISHERS

1. Steve Jones

T–2. Davis Love III

T–2. Tom Lehman

4. John Morse

T–5. Ernie Els

T–5. Jim Furyk

T–7. Scott Hoch

T–7. Vijay Singh

T–7. Ken Green

T–10. Lee Janzen

T–10. Greg Norman

T–10. Colin Montgomerie

LOW SCORERS

First Round: Payne Stewart & Woodie Austin

Second Round: Steve Jones & Greg Norman

Third Round: Tom Lehman

Fourth Round: Scott Hoch

Oakmont Country Club
1927

TOP TEN FINISHERS

1. Tommy Armour

2. Harry Cooper

3. Gene Sarazen

4. Emmett French

5. William Mehlhorn

6. Walter Hagen

T–7. Archie Compston

T–7. Johnny Farrell

T–7. John Golden

T–7. Harry Hampton

LOW SCORERS

First Round: Harry Hampton & Harrison Johnson

Second Round: Tommy Armour

Third Round: Harry Cooper & Arthur Havers

Fourth Round: Al Espinosa

1935

TOP TEN FINISHERS

1. Sam Parks, Jr.

2. Jimmy Thomson

3. Walter Hagen

T–4. Ray Mangrum

T–4. Denny Shute

T–6. Alvin Krueger

T–6. Henry Picard

T–6. Gene Sarazen

T–6. Horton Smith

T–10. Dick Metz

T–10. Paul Runyan

LOW SCORERS

First Round: Al Krueger

Second Round: Ted Turner

Third Round: Henry Picard

Fourth Round: Frank Walsh & Ted Luther

1953

TOP TEN FINISHERS

1. Ben Hogan

2. Sam Snead

3. Lloyd Mangrum

T–4. Pete Cooper

T–4. Jimmy Demaret

T–4. George Fazio

T–7. Ted Kroll

T–7. Dick Metz

T–9. Marty Furgol

T–9. Jay Hebert

T–9. Frank Souchak

LOW SCORERS

First Round: Ben Hogan

Second Round: Sam Snead

Third Round: Dutch Harrison

Fourth Round: Pete Cooper

1962

TOP TEN FINISHERS

1. Jack Nicklaus

2. Arnold Palmer

T–3. Bobby Nichols

T–3. Phil Rodgers

5. Gay Brewer

T–6. Tommy Jacobs

T–6. Gary Player

T–8. Doug Ford

T–8. Gene Littler

T–8. Billy Maxwell

LOW SCORERS

First Round: Gene Littler

Second Round: Arnold Palmer

Third Round: Phil Rodgers & Bo Wininger

Fourth Round: Deane Beman

1973

TOP TEN FINISHERS

1. Johnny Miller

2. John Schlee

3. Tom Weiskopf

T–4. Jack Nicklaus

T–4. Arnold Palmer

T–4. Lee Trevino

T–7. Julius Boros

T–7. Jerry Heard

T–7. Lanny Wadkins

10. Jim Colbert

LOW SCORERS

First Round: Gary Player

Second Round: Gene Borek

Third Round: Jerry Heard

Fourth Round: Johnny Miller

1983

TOP TEN FINISHERS

1. Larry Nelson

2. Tom Watson

3. Gil Morgan

T–4. Seve Ballesteros

T–4. Calvin Peete

6. Hal Sutton

7. Lanny Wadkins

T–8. David Graham

T–8. Ralph Landrum

T–10. Chip Beck

T–10. Andy North

T–10. Craig Stadler

LOW SCORERS

First Round: Seve Ballesteros, John Mahaffey & Bob Murphy

Second Round: Calvin Peete

Third Round: Larry Nelson

Fourth Round: Larry Nelson

1994

TOP TEN FINISHERS

1. Ernie Els

T–2. Colin Montgomerie

T–2. Loren Roberts

4. Curtis Strange

5. John Cook

T–6. Tom Watson

T–6. Greg Norman

T–6. Clark Dennis

T–9. Frank Nobilo

T–9. Jeff Sluman

T–9. Jeff Maggert

T–9. Duffy Waldorf

LOW SCORERS

First Round: Tom Watson

Second Round: Colin Montgomerie, John Cook & David Edwards

Third Round: Loren Roberts

Fourth Round: Duffy Waldorf, Jim McGovern & Sam Torrance

Olympia Fields Country Club
1928

TOP TEN FINISHERS

1. Johnny Farrell

2. Bobby Jones

3. Roland Hancock

T–4. Walter Hagen

T–4. George Von Elm

T–6. Henry Ciuci

T–6. Waldo Crowder

T–6. Ed Dudley

T–6. Bill Leach

T–6. Gene Sarazen

T–6. Denny Shute

T–6. Macdonald Smith

T–6. Joe Turnesa

LOW SCORERS
First Round: Henry Ciuci &
Frank Ball
Second Round: Craig Wood
Third Round: Ed Dudley
Fourth Round: William Mehlhorn

The Olympic Club
1955

TOP TEN FINISHERS
1. Jack Fleck
2. Ben Hogan
T–3. Tommy Bolt
T–3. Sam Snead
T–5. Julius Boros
T–5. Bob Rosburg
T–7. Doug Ford
T–7. Bud Holscher
T–7. Harvie Ward
T–10. Jack Burke
T–10. Mike Souchak

LOW SCORERS
First Round: Tommy Bolt
Second Round: Jack Fleck, Julius
Boros & Sam Snead
Third Round: Bob Rosburg
Fourth Round: Jack Fleck

1966

TOP TEN FINISHERS
1. Billy Casper
2. Arnold Palmer
3. Jack Nicklaus
T–4. Tony Lema
T–4. Dave Marr
6. Phil Rodgers
7. Bobby Nichols
T–8. Wes Ellis
T–8. Johnny Miller
T–8. Mason Rudolph
T–8. Doug Sanders

LOW SCORERS
First Round: Al Mengert
Second Round: Rives McBee
Third Round: Dave Marr
Fourth Round: Billy Casper

1987
TOP TEN FINISHERS
1. Scott Simpson
2. Tom Watson
3. Seve Ballesteros
T–4. Ben Crenshaw
T–4. Bernhard Langer
T–4. Larry Mize
T–4. Curtis Strange
T–4. Bobby Wadkins
T–9. Lennie Clements
T–9. Tommy Nakajima
T–9. Mac O'Grady
T–9. Dan Pohl
T–9. Jim Thorpe

LOW SCORERS
First Round: Ben Crenshaw
Second Round: Tom Watson
Third Round: Keith Clearwater
Fourth Round: Scott Simpson, Jodie
Mudd & Ken Green

Onwentsia Club
1906
TOP TEN FINISHERS
1. Alex Smith
2. Willie Smith
T–3. Laurie Auchterlonie
T–3. James Maiden
5. Willie Anderson
6. Alex Ross
7. Stewart Gardner
T–8. H. Chandler Egan
T–8. Gilbert Nicholls
T–8. Jack Hobens

LOW SCORERS
First Round: Alex Smith, Willie
Smith & Willie Anderson
Second Round: James Maiden
Third Round: Alex Smith
Fourth Round: Willie Smith

Pebble Beach Golf Links
1972
TOP TEN FINISHERS
1. Jack Nicklaus
2. Bruce Crampton
3. Arnold Palmer
T–4. Homero Blancas
T–4. Lee Trevino
6. Kermit Zarley
7. Johnny Miller
8. Tom Weiskopf
T–9. Chi Chi Rodriguez
T–9. Cesar Sanudo

LOW SCORERS
First Round: Jack Nicklaus, Kermit
Zarley, Chi Chi Rodriguez, Orville
Moody, Tom Shaw & Mason Rudolph
Second Round: Arnold Palmer &
Lanny Wadkins
Third Round: Jim Wiechers
Fourth Round: Mason Rudolph

1982
TOP TEN FINISHERS
1. Tom Watson
2. Jack Nicklaus
T–3. Bobby Clampett
T–3. Dan Pohl
T–3. Bill Rogers
T–6. David Graham
T–6. Jay Haas
T–6. Gary Koch
T–6. Lanny Wadkins
T–10. Bruce Devlin
T–10. Calvin Peete

LOW SCORERS

First Round: Bill Rogers &
Bruce Devlin

Second Round: Larry Rinker

Third Round: Lanny Wadkins &
Peter Oosterhuis

Fourth Round: Gary Koch

1992

TOP TEN FINISHERS

1. Tom Kite
2. Jeff Sluman
3. Colin Montgomerie
T–4. Nick Faldo
T–4. Nick Price
T–6. Billy Andrade
T–6. Jay Don Blake
T–6. Bob Gilder
T–6. Mike Hulbert
T–6. Tom Lehman
T–6. Joey Sindelar
T–6. Ian Woosnam

LOW SCORERS

First Round: Gil Morgan

Second Round: Wayne Grady

Third Round: Nick Faldo, Joey
Sindelar & Scott Simpson

Fourth Round: Colin Montgomerie
& Tray Tyner

The Philadelphia Country Club
1939

TOP TEN FINISHERS

1. Byron Nelson
2. Craig Wood
3. Denny Shute
4. Bud Ward
5. Sam Snead
6. Johnny Bulla
T–7. Ralph Guldahl
T–7. Dick Metz

T–9. Ky Laffoon
T–9. Harold McSpaden
T–9. Paul Runyan

LOW SCORERS

First Round: Sam Snead

Second Round: Horton Smith

Third Round: Clayton Heafner

Fourth Round: Byron Nelson

Philadelphia Cricket Club
1907

TOP TEN FINISHERS

1. Alex Ross
2. Gilbert Nicholls
3. Alex Campbell
4. Jack Hobens
T–5. George Low
T–5. Fred McLeod
T–5. Peter Robertson
T–8. David Brown
T–8. Bernard Nicholls
10. Donald Ross

LOW SCORERS

First Round: David Brown

Second Round: Gilbert Nicholls

Third Round: Gilbert Nicholls

Fourth Round: Peter Robertson

1910

TOP TEN FINISHERS

1. Alex Smith
2. John McDermott
3. Macdonald Smith
4. Fred McLeod
T–5. Tom McNamara
T–5. Gilbert Nicholls
7. Jack Hobens
T–8. Tom Anderson Jr.
T–8. H.H. Barker
T–8. Jock Hutchison

LOW SCORERS

First Round: Tom Anderson Jr.

Second Round: Fred McLeod

Third Round: Tom Bonnar

Fourth Round: Macdonald Smith

Riviera Country Club
1948

TOP TEN FINISHERS

1. Ben Hogan
2. Jimmy Demaret
3. Jim Turnesa
4. Bobby Locke
5. Sam Snead
6. Lew Worsham
7. Herman Baron
T–8. Johnny Bulla
T–8. Toney Penna
T–8. Smiley Quick

LOW SCORERS

First Round: Ben Hogan &
Lew Worsham

Second Round: George Schnieter

Third Round: Ben Hogan &
Jimmy Demaret

Fourth Round: Johnny Bulla

St. Louis Country Club
1947

TOP TEN FINISHERS

1. Lew Worsham
2. Sam Snead
T–3. Bobby Locke
T–3. Edward Oliver Jr.
5. Bud Ward
T–6. Jim Ferrier
T–6. Vic Ghezzi
T–6. Leland Gibson
T–6. Ben Hogan
T–6. Johnny Palmer
T–6. Paul Runyan

LOW SCORERS
First Round: Chick Harbert
Second Round: Jimmy Demaret
Third Round: James McHale Jr.
Fourth Round: Vic Ghezzi

Scioto Country Club
1926

TOP TEN FINISHERS
1. Bobby Jones
2. Joe Turnesa
T–3. Leo Diegel
T–3. Johnny Farrell
T–3. William Mehlhorn
T–3. Gene Sarazen
7. Walter Hagen
8. Willie Hunter Jr.
T–9. Tommy Armour
T–9. Willie Klein
T–9. Macdonald Smith
T–9. Dan Williams

LOW SCORERS
First Round: William Mehlhorn
Second Round: Jack Forrester
Third Round: Macdonald Smith
Fourth Round: Gene Sarazen

Shinnecock Hills Golf Club
1896

TOP TEN FINISHERS
1. James Foulis
2. Horace Rawlins
3. Joe Lloyd
T–4. George Douglas
T–4. A.W. Smith
T–6. John Shippen
T–6. H.J. Whigham
8. Willie Tucker
9. R.B. Wilson
10. Alfred Ricketts

LOW SCORERS
First Round: Joe Lloyd
Second Round: James Foulis

1986

TOP TEN FINISHERS
1. Ray Floyd
T–2. Chip Beck
T–2. Lanny Wadkins
T–4. Hal Sutton
T–4. Lee Trevino
T–6. Ben Crenshaw
T–6. Payne Stewart
T–8. Bernhard Langer
T–8. Mark McCumber
T–8. Jack Nicklaus
T–8. Bob Tway

LOW SCORERS
First Round: Bob Tway
Second Round: Joey Sindelar
Third Round: Hal Sutton & Mike Reid
Fourth Round: Chip Beck, Lanny Wadkins & Mark Calcavecchia

1995

TOP TEN FINISHERS
1. Corey Pavin
2. Greg Norman
3. Tom Lehman
T–4. Neal Lancaster
T–4. Jeff Maggert
T–4. Bill Glasson
T–4. Jay Haas
T–4. Davis Love III
T–4. Phil Mickelson
T–10. Frank Nobilo
T–10. Vijay Singh
T–10. Bob Tway

LOW SCORERS
First Round: Nick Price
Second Round: Greg Norman & Bernhard Langer
Third Round: Tom Lehman
Fourth Round: Neal Lancaster

Skokie Country Club
1922

TOP TEN FINISHERS
1. Gene Sarazen
T–2. John Black
T–2. Bobby Jones
4. William Mehlhorn
5. Walter Hagen
6. George Duncan
7. Leo Diegel
T–8. Mike Brady
T–8. John Golden
T–8. Jock Hutchison

LOW SCORERS
First Round: Walter Hagen
Second Round: Lloyd Gullickson
Third Round: Bobby Jones
Fourth Round: Gene Sarazen

Southern Hills Country Club
1958

TOP TEN FINISHERS
1. Tommy Bolt
2. Gary Player
3. Julius Boros
4. Gene Littler
T–5. Walter Burkemo
T–5. Bob Rosburg
T–7. Jay Hebert
T–7. Don January
T–7. Dick Metz
T–10. Ben Hogan
T–10. Tommy Jacobs
T–10. Frank Stranahan

LOW SCORERS

First Round: Tommy Bolt, Julius Boros & Dick Metz

Second Round: Gary Player

Third Round: Gene Littler

Fourth Round: Jay Hebert & Bob Goetz

1977

TOP TEN FINISHERS

1. Hubert Green
2. Lou Graham
3. Tom Weiskopf
4. Tom Purtzer
T–5. Jay Haas
T–5. Gary Jacobsen
T–7. Lyn Lott
T–7. Terry Diehl
T–7. Tom Watson
T–10. Rod Funseth
T–10. Al Geiberger
T–10. Mike McCullough
T–10. Jack Nicklaus
T–10. Peter Oosterhuis
T–10. Gary Player

LOW SCORERS

First Round: Hubert Green, Tom Purtzer, Terry Diehl, Rod Funseth, Grier Jones, Forentino Molina & Larry Nelson

Second Round: Hubert Green, Gary Player & Jim Simons

Third Round: Don Padgett

Fourth Round: Jerry McGee

The Country Club
1913

TOP TEN FINISHERS

1. Francis Ouimet
2. Harry Vardon
3. Edward Ray

T–4. James Barnes
T–4. Walter Hagen
T–4. Macdonald Smith
T–4. Louis Tellier
8. John McDermott
9. Herbert Strong
10. Pat Doyle

LOW SCORERS

First Round: Macdonald Smith & Alex Ross

Second Round: Edward Ray

Third Round: Pat Doyle

Fourth Round: Matt Campbell & Louid Tellier

1963

TOP TEN FINISHERS

1. Julius Boros
T–2. Jacky Cupit
T–2. Arnold Palmer
4. Paul Harney
T–5. Bruce Crampton
T–5. Tony Lema
T–5. Billy Maxwell
T–8. Walter Burkemo
T–8. Gary Player
10. Dan Sikes

LOW SCORERS

First Round: Bob Gadja

Second Round: Arnold Palmer & Dow Finserwald

Third Round: Paul Harney & Dan Sikes

Fourth Round: Julius Boros, Gary Player & Gene Littler

1988

TOP TEN FINISHERS

1. Curtis Strange
2. Nick Faldo
T–3. Mark O'Meara

T–3. Steve Pate
T–3. D.A. Weibring
T–6. Paul Azinger
T–6. Scott Simpson
T–8. Bob Gilder
T–8. Fuzzy Zoeller
T–10. Fred Couples
T–10. Payne Stewart

LOW SCORERS

First Round: Bob Gilder, Sandy Lyle & Mike Nicolette

Second Round: Scott Simpson

Third Round: Mark O'Meara

Fourth Round: Peter Jacobsen

Winged Foot Golf Club
1929

TOP TEN FINISHERS

1. Bobby Jones
2. Al Espinosa
T–3. Gene Sarazen
T–3. Denny Shute
T–5. Tommy Armour
T–5. George Von Elm
7. Henry Ciuci
T–8. Leo Deigel
T–8. Peter O'Hara
10. Horton Smith

LOW SCORERS

First Round: Bobby Jones

Second Round: George Von Elm

Third Round: Bobby Jones

Fourth Round: James Barnes

1959

TOP TEN FINISHERS

1. Billy Casper
2. Bob Rosburg
T–3. Claude Harmon
T–3. Mike Souchak
T–5. Doug Ford

T–5. Arnold Palmer

T–5. Ernie Vossler

T–8. Ben Hogan

T–8. Sam Snead

10. Dick Knight

LOW SCORERS

First Round: Ben Hogan, Dow Finsterwald, Gene Littler & Dick Knight

Second Round: Billy Casper & Chick Harbert

Third Round: Bob Rosburg & Sam Snead

Fourth Round: Bob Rosburg, Claude Harmon & Mike Souchak

1974

TOP TEN FINISHERS

1. Hale Irwin

2. Forrest Fezler

T–3. Lou Graham

T–3. Bert Yancey

T–5. Jim Colbert

T–5. Arnold Palmer

T–5. Tom Watson

T–8. Tom Kite

T–8. Gary Player

T–10. Brian Allin

T–10. Jack Nicklaus

LOW SCORERS

First Round: Gary Player

Second Round: Hubert Green

Third Round: Tom Watson & Jim Colbert

Fourth Round: Al Geiberger

1984

TOP TEN FINISHERS

1. Fuzzy Zoeller

2. Greg Norman

3. Curtis Strange

T–4. Johnny Miller

T–4. Jim Thorpe

6. Hale Irwin

T–7. Peter Jacobsen

T–7. Mark O'Meara

T–9. Fred Couples

T–9. Lee Trevino

LOW SCORERS

First Round: Jim Thorpe, Hale Irwin, Hubert Green & Mike Donald

Second Round: Fuzzy Zoeller

Third Round: Tim Simpson

Fourth Round: Peter Jacobsen

Worcester Country Club
1925

TOP TEN FINISHERS

1. Willie MacFarlane

2. Bobby Jones

T–3. Johnny Farrell

T–3. Francis Ouimet

T–5. Walter Hagen

T–5. Gene Sarazen

7. Mike Brady

8. Leo Diegel

T–9. Laurie Ayton

T–9. Al Espinosa

LOW SCORERS

First Round: Francis Ouimet

Second Round: Willie MacFarlane

Third Round: Johnny Farrell

Fourth Round: John Golden